The push and pull of political, social, and emotional forces

can tug our muscular systems

out of alignment with our hopes, dreams, and values.

Disorientation.

The pressure of oppression, pressing our lungs so tightly

that we cannot inspire fully or be fully inspired.

Forming bodies into false impressions

of self and other.

Fear, isolation, insecurity.

Yet as long as we are alive and breathing and willing

we can become re-oriented and re-aligned.

We can reshape our muscular systems by

changing our belief systems.

And vice versa.

Contents

Thanks to Suzanne Richman, my mentor, advisor, and editor throughout this last year of writing.

Thanks to all of the faculty and students of Goddard College who helped make this work possible.

Thanks also to The Strozzi Institute, The Florida School of Massage, Mariah Marks and my wonderfully supportive community in Gainesville, Fl.

Preface

When I was in elementary school, my teacher made my classmates and I stand outside with our arms stretched out for several minutes. It was obvious that we were all uncomfortable, but she wouldn't let us put our arms down. "This is what Jesus went through for your sins," she explained.

I went to a Catholic school.

I've always been the kind of person who is deeply impacted by my environment. I feel things very strongly. I take in other people's pain and I feel their joy. I can sense the trees whimpering when I watch a forest being clear-cut. Sometimes the full moon makes my heart race so fast that I've had to go to the hospital. So when my young imagination was filled with fearful images of the divine- of hell and damnation, of sin and mortality- my whole body was overtaken by a deep and crippling anxiety. Of course, as a child I didn't have the insight to realize how sensitive I was or to question what was being handed to me as truth. I just believed the stories that I was told and I accepted the feelings that came along with them as normal. But it wasn't very long before I realized that other people were not having the same experience of life.

~~~~~~

I remember my South Florida childhood quite vividly, those carefree days before anxiety took hold of me: the summer water balloon fights, street hockey pick-up games, and secret forts in the woods. My parents gave my brother and I the freedom to roam the neighborhood, which allowed us to explore and to discover pieces of ourselves that were hidden under rocks and in pine forests. The possibilities felt endless. It was really the best childhood I could have asked for.

One afternoon, when I was in middle school, my best friend invited me to "youth group" at a local evangelical church. Kickball and free snacks sounded great, so I agreed to tag along. Very quickly, this youth group became my life.

It was a blast. I have so many fond memories from dodge ball games, awkward crushes, concerts, and mission trips around the world. Yet it all came at an expense. This church was, and still is, a haven of evangelical fundamentalism. Fundamentalism is predicated on the idea that there is only one path and deviating from that path is worthy of punishment: everlasting, torturous punishment. The expansiveness I felt as a child was quickly replaced by the narrow road.

Shortly after gaining my trust, one of the pastors explained to me that all Catholics go to hell, warning that my family's eternal lives were in danger because they still went to Catholic Church. This news terrified me, so I asked my parents to switch churches. My mom was hesitant at first. She was a very devoted Catholic. But when it comes down to it, she is more devoted to being a good mom. So my family took a leap of faith and jumped from Catholicism to evangelicalism.

Evangelical Christian churches, like the one I went to, have syphoned the mystery of the gospel story down to a simple formula. The steps to salvation begin with admitting you are a sinner and repenting before God. Then you simply ask for forgiveness and you are saved, as long as you do it *with a pure heart*. It's supposed to be a one-time deal, but I got saved at least five times, maybe more. We were constantly being reminded by the church to question the purity of our hearts. I took this seriously, learning to constantly question and second-guess myself. This left me frequently wondering whether I was truly saved. The rhetoric all around me was clear and constant: you could die at any moment and if you are not right with God you will be tortured and burn in hell forever. This idea wasn't just planted in my head; it was drilled into my head. The story I was being told over and over again was about my inherent unworthiness and God's plan to save me from the hell I deserve if I repent correctly. To me, this was not good news; it was tragic, and I believed every word of it.

Questioning it was out of the question. Even thinking about questioning it was out of the question. Honest inquiry was demonized as "doubt creeping in," allowing the devil too strong of a foothold.

These stories of hell, damnation, and original sin were told to me over and over again throughout my middle and high school years. This set of beliefs, paired with unrealistic expectations about morality, was just too much for my vulnerable young soul to handle. I was utterly terrified that all of my friends and family, possibly even myself, may be thrown into the lake of fire at any moment. I became quite obsessed with spiritual and moral purity. What was most confusing to me is that while I believed all of this with intense conviction, no one else really seemed to.

Despite the continual admonition to take every word of the bible literally, my conviction to do so was seen by my family and my church as abnormal. My behavior became problematic. I'd like to illustrate this point by quoting a piece from an article that I wrote for Geez Magazine in 2012:

> After church, we drove in our family minivan to the closest fast-food drive-through for a deliciously unscrupulous lunch of 99-cent chilidogs. Just as my parents were about to place our order, it hit me: I had forgotten to tithe! [To those not versed in Christian lingo, this means ritualistically giving money to the church]. I confessed immediately to my mom, who was, disturbingly more interested in finishing the order than in the gravity of my trespass. Distraught by my parent's reaction, I threatened not to

eat my chilidog until they drove me back
to church.

I had read the story. That couple in
the Book of Acts made the same mistake
and God struck them dead on the spot.

This was the first of the 'episodes'
that eventually led my parents to make
me seek treatment. I was diagnosed with
Obsessive Compulsive Disorder (OCD),
a condition that results from severe
anxiety and fear. But I didn't quite
understand. I read the Bible and I
believed it, and my punishment for such
a faithful interpretation was a psychiatric
label and an intense fear of life... I don't
think anyone else really believed in the
eternal damnation of hell, because if they
did, they would have ended up in
therapy too. (2012, p. 33)

It seems glaringly clear to me; when I believed in a
god that threatened to kill me if I stepped out of line, and
eternally torment me if I wasn't "saved," I was terrified.
This terror was reflected in my body through compulsions,
convulsions, twitches, and literal paralysis. The moment I
stopped believing in hell and absolutism, I was able to
throw away my medicine and I have not experienced a
symptom since. Not even once. It's been over 10 years.

It wasn't easy to let go of the religious teachings that had such a gripping effect on me. But by the time I left my hometown and home church to go to college, I was ready for relief. I was sick of living in fear. Luckily I landed in the liberal town of Gainesville, Florida, were I was exposed to various forms of progressive Christianity. I quickly came to realize that there are varying interpretations of the bible that starkly contrast one another. With an eager heart I latched onto the intellectual reading of the scriptures that these churches taught. I was able to free my mind, which in turn freed my body from the grip of anxiety.

It was really scary and disorienting to shift my worldview, and I was shamed for it by my church back home. It felt like purgatory, as if my whole body was being stretched between heaven and hell, right and wrong, confusion and clarity. Yet I can't overstate how immediate the shift inside of me was as soon as I gave up my belief in hell. This was the piece of the story that was responsible for my obsessive thoughts and crippling fear. Letting it go was everything.

Several years later at a garage sale I stumbled across a book about OCD called *The Boy Who Couldn't Stop Washing*. As I flipped through the pages of this worn text I discovered an intriguing appendix wedged into the back pages like an afterthought. It was titled *The Religious Perspective: The Catholic Church and OCD*. To my surprise, yet not surprisingly at all, there is a long and well-documented history of OCD symptomology among Catholics (Rapaport, 1991).

The book cites documentation from the Catholic Church dating back to the 16th century, which describes a curious condition called scrupulosity. It was apparently so common that priests were trained in how to counsel parishioners suffering from it. The 16th century list of symptoms mirrors the 21st century symptomology of OCD with exact precision.

Scrupulosity: Persistent concern with thought, word, or deed.

OCD: Persistent intrusive idea, thought, or impulse.

Scrupulosity: Thoughts cause uneasiness of distress.

OCD: Ritual or thought causes distress.

Scrupulosity: Person compelled and obsessional thoughts.

OCD: Thoughts or actions performed with obsessive compulsion.

Scrupulosity: Occurs in healthy person.

OCD: Not due to another mental or
physical disturbance.

(Rapaport, 1991, p. 260)

~~~~~~

The doctrines of Catholicism and the fundamentals
of Evangelical Christianity are considered "normal" by
many people. But to me these represent devastating and
traumatizing belief systems. All these years later the ideas
that were drilled into my head are still there, haunting me
in unexpected ways, pressing triggers I didn't even know I
had. Throughout this book, I will trace out how these
stories still tend to live in my body, and describe the
practices that have helped me to somatically reorient my
worldview, and further loosen the grip of anxiety.

The proceeding chapters will outline some of the
ways that bodies shape beliefs and beliefs shape bodies.
This dynamic interplay of physical and social forces is too
often ignored in Western culture. Bodies are living
organisms that are in a constant state of flux and flow,
contraction and expansion, constantly shifting shape in
response to the social world. We are characters physically
embedded in a grand narrative. Yet we also have the
power to become the author, and authors have the power
to change the story. Throughout this book, I am suggesting

that a somatically-oriented shift in perspective is necessary for the creation of free minds, free bodies, and a free world.

Chapter 1

What is Somatics?

"All muscular contractions contain the history and meaning of their origin."

-Wilhelm Reich

Buried Memories

"Do you hear that?" he asked, as I was massaging his back. "Hear what?" I said. We were in a second story apartment in Florida; windows open to cool the room. "Oh nothing. It must be coming from outside." I continued working my hands into his rigid back muscles. I had just finished massage school and had been practicing primarily on my friends. I've learned that when I massage friends, as opposed to strangers, they are much more likely to speak up if something out of the ordinary happens. "There it is again. You really don't hear that?" I heard nothing. "What do you hear?" I finally asked. "The accordion. It's so loud. How can you not hear it?"

After discussing this mysterious sound for a few minutes, we realized that it only appeared when I pressed deeply into the particular muscle of my friend's back that supports his own accordion's strap. Whether the rhomboids or the traps, I don't specifically recall, but his reaction was so immediate and particular that it was like pressing the play button on a radio.

This was not the first of the peculiar experiences that have taken place while massaging friends. When I was still in massage school, I had an experience that would catalyze my ongoing exploration of the body's innate wisdom. As I was massaging my best friend, she suddenly began crying and whimpering as I touched into her sternocleidomastoid muscle, which is a muscle that wraps the throat. In shock, I stopped the session. She explained that by putting my hand there I had triggered an unexpected memory of a past relationship. After a moment of processing, she asked me to continue, so I did, gently, and the tears poured out. The session left her feeling cathartic. Through conversations with other classmates, I realized that several others were also having these kinds of experiences.

~~~~~~

In *The Body Remembers*, Babette Rothschild explains that because our senses are the first contact we have with the outer world, all memory begins with sensory input. For this reason, "It might be something seen, heard, tasted, or smelled… that sets the flashback in motion… Sensory messages from muscles and connective tissue that remember a particular position, action, or intention can be the source of a trigger" (2000, p. 45).

My friends were experiencing small flashbacks of very particular moments in time when my fingers pressed into the muscles that held those memories. The emerging field of somatics begins with the assumption that our bodies, as well as our minds, contain our personal stories: all of the experiences, histories, and emotions that collectively shape our personalities and our muscles. Because so much of our story lives in our bodies, shifting our awareness to our bodies can open up a reservoir of hidden wisdom and cause a deeply embodied shift in perspective. I'm interested in the way our unconscious muscular responses, structured by past experiences, memories, and traumas, still play an integral role in our current lives and relationships on both a micro and macro level. And I'm ultimately interested in how our less beneficial somatic narratives can be challenged and changed.

The Feeling of Emotions

Shortly before the turn of the last century, the philosopher William James made an intriguing observation about the human body and emotions:

> If we fancy some strong emotion and
> then try to abstract from our
> consciousness of all the feelings of its
> bodily symptoms, we find we have
> nothing left behind, no "mind stuff" out
> of which the emotion can be constituted,
> and that a cold and neutral state of
> intellectual perception is all that
> remains... What kind of emotion of fear

would be left if the feeling neither of
quickened heart-beats nor of shallow
breathing, neither of trembling lips nor
of weakened limbs, neither of gooseflesh
nor of visceral stirrings, were present, it
is quite impossible for me to think. Can
one fancy a state of rage and picture no
ebullition of the chest, no flushing of the
face, no dilatation of the nostrils, no
clenching of the teeth, no impulse to
vigorous action, but in their stead limp
muscles, calm breathing, and a placid
face? (James, 1890)

The sensory organization of the body is made up of
the exteroceptive and interoceptive nerves. Exteroceptive
nerves receive and transmit information from outside the
body, while interoceptive nerves receive and transmit
information from inside the body, via the viscera, muscles,
and connective tissue (Rothschild, 2000). These systems of
nerves are broken down into further categories. One of the
categories that is surely familiar to us all is called the
internal sense. These are the bodily sensations that James
gives voice to: heart rate, respiration, temperature, blood
flow, muscle tension, etc. These internal sense perceptions
inform the biological basis of emotions.

What we sometimes refer to as "emotions" can be
thought of simply as the words we use to describe these
bodily sensations or feelings. A quickly beating heart, for

example, may be called panic or anxiety. The quivering of the lips accompanied by watering eyes and sudden inhalations may be understood as sadness. A churning of the stomach may be referred to as nervousness. These bodily responses are often triggered before cognitive thought catches up.

I'm constantly fascinated by language, by the terms and phrases that tend to be taken for granted. When closely analyzed, words can offer so much insight into the rich history of their associations and meanings. The word "emotion," as you might guess, has early associations with motion. The Latin word *emovere* means, "to move out." In 12th century French *emouvoir* meant, "to stir up," and in 16th century French emotion began to refer to broader social stirrings or political agitations. It wasn't until the 1800s that the word emotion began to refer loosely to any sort of feeling (Harper, 2016). The word "feeling," which often gets used interchangeably with the word "emotion," refers directly to this felt sense that I am talking about.

If what we feel internally is a direct response to stimuli, then we don't necessarily have a choice in what bodily responses, or feelings, are triggered. If someone yells at me to get off of the road as I am biking, I am going to feel a sudden rush of energy in my body, and interpret it as fear or anger. The repression of feelings, in contrast, is an intentional process of cutting off, numbing, or ignoring the sensations rising in the body in response to stimuli. I will talk at length about repression later, but for now I want to point out that stimuli, and thus feelings, are not something we can simply avoid. Yet as we build up an awareness of the emotional forces that enter our lives and shape our worlds, we can learn to respond with choice, instead of letting these surges of feeling control us.

Despite the inevitability of human feeling, we live amongst so many narratives that devalue the felt sense. The narrative of masculinity is perhaps the most pervasive example. Yet the narrative of rationalism that dominates Western culture is also one that devalues feelings, and their associated emotions, throwing them into the same category as superstition and speculation. Yet these feelings that arise in response to stimuli are so human. They are so ingrained into our very being and body that it is curious to me how Western culture has managed to dismiss their influence so readily. By eradicating feeling from the human experience, masculinity, rationalism, and even science have taught us to leave our bodies behind. This is of course influenced heavily by Christianity's view of the body as evil and dangerous.

The marriage of religion and rationalism has created a false dualism between body and mind that is based on the narrative that feelings are primitive, dangerous, and to be overcome by rational thought and moral purity. According to rationalists, feelings get in the way of clear-headed thinking. To moral purists, feelings stir up temptation. This is the world we have inherited in the West. It's not subtle; it's extremely pervasive. Yet it so often goes unnoticed or unquestioned. Somatics challenges this narrative by tuning into the body and beginning to understand feeling and emotion not only as inherently human, but also as inherently insightful.

Our senses are our first contact with our external environments. Messages are received and transmitted through feelings registered by the nervous system: that knife is sharp, don't touch it. Often these messages make it to the brain and get stored as learned information. Yet some memories don't rely on the brain for recall. We make use of this kind of memory every day. Walking for example, is not something that we are consciously thinking about when we do it, though at some point we all had to learn the steps. This form of memory, which is called implicit memory, and is sometimes casually referred to as muscle memory, takes place outside of conscious control.

"The knife is sharp, don't touch!" This isn't something that we have to consciously remind ourselves every time we see a knife. In fact, if we have been cut by a knife in the past and felt the associated pain, our muscles may tense up immediately at even the sight of a knife.

Neuroscientist Antonio Damasio's theory of somatic markers is based on this implicit wisdom of the body. In stark contrast to the popular idea that emotions get in the way of rational thought, he proposes that emotional reactions may actually provide useful information that may be out of our conscious reach. What we can "feel in our bones" or what our "gut feelings" may be telling us, according to Damasio and a growing number of neuroscientists, may actually contain accurate and relevant information (1994).

There are obvious examples of this that we can all relate to. If I got desperately ill eating a certain food, my body might strongly advise that I don't eat that food again by feeling a sense of nausea and disgust when I smell it. In the same way, if I lived with a roommate that made my life miserable years ago, and am thinking about living with that person again, I may have an "gut feeling" that it's a bad idea. But if the rent is really cheap and lots of time has passed and she has a really cute dog and the house is perfect, etc., then I may be tempted to override this feeling and discount it as irrational. It is of course the case that things may actually be very different now. But the point is that the feeling stirring up inside of me is based on lived experience and is offering me insight into the past, specifically into how the past felt, which is something that the rational mind can't offer.

Traumatic Memory

More than just memories or past emotions are being collected in our muscles and tissue in response to stimuli. The energy, or intensity, of these sensory responses is also felt and stored. A rush of blood to the extremities, an increasing heart rate, clenched or spasming muscles responding to threat, all have an energetic component. I use the term energy loosely to encompass all of the fluids and feelings that are moving through the body. This is the "stirring" or the "motion" of emotions.

The field of trauma studies has been revolutionized in recent years both by studies in neuroscience and by those who are looking towards the body for answers. One of the leading questions that has sparked this emerging research is the question of why wild animals don't seem to ever get traumatized (Levine, 1997). Observation has shown that when animals in the wild experience trauma, which they do quite often, they tend to be able to return to normal functioning almost immediately: sleeping, having sex, and grazing for food. We know that these three particular functions- sleep, reproduction, and hunger/digestion- are usually deactivated in humans by a traumatic event and often take long periods of time to re-activate. Why are non-human animals able to move seamlessly through this process? The answer is in the body.

When an animal experiences trauma, whether it's being chased through the woods, shot at, attacked, or watching a herd member get eaten alive, their bodies go into fight or flight mode. This is also true for human animals. Yet wild animals have no social norms or expectations telling them not to fight back, or not to run- as most domesticated humans tend to have. So they run, or they fight back.

A third option for a nervous system response is to freeze. This is an intelligent response that the body initiates if it assesses that fighting or fleeing is not possible. In these situations, the body shuts down, essentially forcing the animal to play dead, to disassociate. In this state, the animal feels no pain and often won't remember the situation. This is why extremely traumatic events, most notably sexual assault, can be literally impossible to escape (as the body shuts down), and can sometimes even be hidden from memory.

After wild animals get locked into freeze mode and then begin to "thaw", they have been observed to shake, to make loud noises, and tremble. Then they graze for food, have sex and fall asleep. How do they transition so quickly? The intensity of the experience gets released from the body through their spasms and tears. Stress hormones literally get flushed out through the sweat glands and tears ducts, and allow the nervous system to return immediately to a parasympathetic state. The buildup of energy and contracted muscles become released and relaxed by shaking, or running, or fighting (Levine, 1997).

Trauma can be understood as a cycle of stimuli, response, and release. Yet too often in human animals, we don't make it to the third step of this cycle. We tend to hold all of the intensity and energy of the traumatic experience in our bodies without releasing it. There are a few reasons for this. First of all, it is generally not appropriate, acceptable, or even safe to fight back when attacked or threatened. The same goes for fleeing. The other major factor that distinguishes wild animals from human animals is the development of our frontal cortex. This is the part of our brain that allows us to rationalize: don't fight back, don't cry, everything's going to be ok. Animals without a frontal cortex don't have this forethought; they just respond. In humans, in our current society, being able to rationalize and predetermine our actions is incredibly useful. But if wild animals are enslaved to their instincts, human animals are enslaved to our rational minds. Each has their own set of benefits and downfalls.

When serious threats come in the form of huge trucks running us off roads, gun shots in the distance, politicians threatening to deport whole groups of people or take away access to food or housing, our nervous systems may be in a perpetual state of panic. In our current human society, we can't just run away like wild animals can.

I will talk more in the concluding chapter about how various practitioners are discovering ways to support the release of traumatic energy through the body for the sake of healing. It's fascinating and groundbreaking work. But for now I want to continue with a short history of this emerging field known as somatics.

Somatic Thinking

Somatics is the study of the inner and outer life of the body. It's the study of how bodies exist in relationship to each other, of why we are attracted to some things and repelled by other things. It's the study of feeling, emotion, joy, pain, love, and death. The field of somatics is informed by the life sciences, and by psychology, but it is categorically different from both because of its approach. Somatics begins with the subjective inner experience of the body and moves outward. This first person observation of the self (proprioception) allows for critically different insights than third person observation is capable of.

In the search for universals and commonalities, the objective sciences look at bodies from the outside, detached from the subjective internal process of the individual. When this is the single vantage point from which bodies are analyzed and categorized, so much gets missed. Bodies become viewed as predictable machines instead of as what we are- people made of complex stories with ever-shifting internal responses to a dynamic external world. Somatics is the study of the body as experienced from within. *Somatics is a shift in perspective.*

It is an attempt to bring a *wholeness of being* into the conversations about bodies, a conversation that has been too long dominated by objective science and impersonal observation. Bodies are not static: they are in a continual mode of change and self-regulation, constantly expanding and contracting, growing and shrinking. The sensory-

25

motor system regulates this constant motion as it takes in stimuli. Bodies are always acting and reacting, sensing and responding, internalizing and mobilizing. Much of this flux and flow is involuntary and outside of conscious control, and much of it is not. The power and promise of somatics is to expand possibility by bringing our reactions into full consciousness for the purpose of shifting involuntary responses into voluntary choices. The goal of somatics is to restore a wholeness of being, understanding that *being* is an active verb, not a static existence.

The term somatics was coined in 1976 by an existential philosopher named Thomas Hanna. Though the field had already been evolving for many years, Hanna's book *Bodies in Revolt: A Primer in Somatic Thinking,* was the first attempt to establish a unified framework that would capture this emerging movement.

I am looking at a copy of the book right now. It's worn and marked up. The color of the pages has faded to a musty off-white. It smells as old as it is. It's a comforting sort of smell, reminiscent of a quant and quiet library, like the library I am sitting in now. As I am typing these words and underlining quotes from Hanna's book I am on the campus of the University of Florida. This is the place where Hanna gave birth to the field of somatics. He was the founder of the *University of Florida's* Philosophy Department in the 1960's. This locale where I am writing from is the vantage point from where he wrote this primer that I now hold in my hands.

It's a strange and curious sensation to be connected to place in this way. I have a unique sense of Hanna's words because of what I know about this place, from a mix of historical knowledge of the political climate that was present then to a felt experience of the climate that is present now. The book is written with a tangible sense of optimism and a deeply held belief in an inevitable shift towards somatic thinking that Hanna believed would characterize the coming decades. Gainesville, Florida, where the university resides, had been deemed the "Berkeley of the South" around the time of Hanna's writing. The massive amount of students protesting, dreaming, and organizing was evidence of a shifting culture, a shedding of constricting social values, a freeing of bodily impulses, and a fresh alignment of desire and action.

To Hanna, somatics would be an expansive field that would complement many existing fields. In this first book, Hanna proposed a somatically oriented shift in perspective that would permeate the life sciences, psychology, politics, social theory, etc. Later in his career he syphoned his ideas down to formulate a program of physical therapy for releasing involuntary muscular constrictions. This process is outlined in his best-selling book *Somatics: Reawakening the Mind's Control of Movement, Flexibility, and Health.*

Somatics is largely based on existential and phenomenological inquiry. According to Thomas Hanna, somatics is "a field of study dealing with somatic phenomena: i.e., the human being as experienced by himself from inside the body" (Hanna, 1986). Somatic thinking has indeed permeated many fields. Psychology, neuroscience, cultural studies, queer theory, literary studies, and anthropology are just a few examples of where somatic thinking has had influence. The applications vary from field to field but are all based on the shared premise that the body is an essential component of what it means to be human.

Much of this book will draw from phenomenology. As a philosophy that is concerned with one's perception and internal sense of the outer world, it fits quite well into a study like this. Phenomenology is hard to define because philosophers don't share much consensus about its application or approach (Osborne, 2007). My understanding, and what I take from the tradition, is that knowledge is primarily found in the unfolding of phenomenon as it happens. It is a philosophy based on pure observation, in an attempt to rid one's mind of biased interpretations or assumptions. It places a profound trust on the direct experience of the individual. If I am looking at a tree, my philosophical inquiry of the tree begins with my observation and experience of the tree: "The bark feels hard and flakey." This is different from an observation based on what I have been taught about trees: "That's a beautiful tree that God made," or "That's a dangerous invasive."

I have also become particularly fascinated with the work of Sara Ahmed, author of *The Cultural Politics of Emotion* and *Queer Phenomenology*. Her work resonates with me because of her inquiry into the social realm of the body. She explores how social stigma often results from a learned misreading of the "other" and a misinterpretation of our own bodily reactions to the "other." Ahmed's phenomenology involves a critical examination of our own perception and biases.

Somatics, in the larger sense, is not only about individual bodies, but it is also about bodies in relationship to one another. In an existential sense, I would even consider the possibility that there may not really be such a thing as an "individual body." A feeling that you are experiencing may produce a feeling in my own body, and vice versa. Too often, personal identity consists of little more than a set of barriers constructed to distinguish you from me. This gets to the heart of why somatics is so important to me. This world is a hard place to be in a body. There's so much pain, oppression, trauma, and stress that we have no choice but to build up defenses against the vulnerability of life. We tense our muscles and close ourselves off. We learn patterns of movement that keep us protected, distant, and separate. Sometimes those patterns and defenses serve us and protect us well. Yet other times, maybe even most of the time, they don't serve us, but instead hinder us from truly connecting, from truly feeling, and from truly being alive. Thus, somatics is also about bringing awareness to the defenses we've built up so that we can learn to instead open toward the world and re-connect to the larger body of existence.

Your body, my body, and everybody is wrapped up in this thing we call life. We recycle the air together. We sleep under the same moon, with the same sorts of spinning thoughts circling in our minds as we wonder who we are and why we are here. We wake up to the same sun and feel the same gusts of wind. The same source of gravity weighs on our spines, and the same dirt and rocks shape the contours of our feet.

Many of us in the West however, tend to be quite disconnected from our bodies, lacking a basic awareness of what's happening internally. This severely limits our capacity for responding to the world in an intentional way. The emotional stirrings inside of our bodies either become jumbled and confused, overwhelming the senses, or we learn to block them out altogether.

In order to survive the constant stimuli of everyday, we often learn to close ourselves off, limiting our body's capacity for expansion and growth. Ron Kurtz, one of the pioneers in the field of somatics, puts it this way:

> With the number of family and work demands, placed upon us, in the limited space of crowded cities, survival takes precedence. What this means is that from early childhood, we begin to learn that

> holding back compromising feeling is
> safer than allowing free synchronous
> pulsing. This holding is most often
> manifest as rings of muscles and fascial
> tension in areas between the major
> segments of the body. (Kurtz, 1976, p. 23)

As we involuntarily tense our muscles to block the flow of sensation, blood supply is reduced, leading to a collection of toxic waste, increasing the likelihood of spasm and stasis. Over time, if this tensing becomes habitual, our muscles learn these patterns and harden in an attempt to splint the area from pain or spasm (Kurtz, 1976). Eventually this chronic muscle tension becomes structural; it becomes who we are.

I tend to hold a lot of emotional energy in my chest. The wide array of analogies relating to the heart are no coincidence. As one of our most vital organs of life, it represents great vulnerability. It takes trust to "open the heart." I once had a somatic teacher tell me that instead of referring to the ribcage as a "cage," there are other cultures that refer to it as a "rib basket." These small semantic distinctions make a huge difference in how we perceive the world. Is our heart something that is guarded and locked away in a cage, or is it something that is supported and held in a basket?

A chest that is collapsed, or deflated, can often be indicative of a lack of emotional vitality. Such a person's life may be characterized by a literal lack of inspiration, as taking full breaths become too difficult. By limiting the breath, pain and vulnerability can be avoided. What I am trying to emphasize here is that one's physical body and emotional life, as regulated by the sensory motor system, exists in a kind of feedback loop: sense and response are functionally inseparable (Hanna, 1986). This has become more obvious to me the more I have studied somatics and paid attention to my own body.

In contrast to a collapsed chest, an over-expanded chest remains chronically inflated, forming protective muscular barriers around the heart and lungs. This represents a fear of softening, of letting go. It indicates a rigid position in life, both ideologically and physically. Ron Kurtz describes his work with people who hold their chests in this way:

> The more held and expanded the chest,
> the less fluid the personality. The most
> striking observation about these
> individuals is their inability to exhale, to
> release the air contained within. The chest
> resists collapsing. When they do, whether
> through encouragement or the application
> of direct force, deep sobbing can result.
> (Kurtz, 1976, p. 81)

Thinking about bodies in this way, as active and alive, can be challenging for people whose perception has been shaped by Western thought. Thomas Hanna wanted to use a word other than "body" when speaking of the human experience because "it is easier to recognize new wine when it is put into new bottles" (Hanna, 1970, p. 35). Hanna's original description of his chosen term "soma" is beautifully poetic and worth quoting at length:

> Somas are unique things, which are yearning, hoping, suffering, tensing, paling, cringing, doubting, despairing. Human somas are convulsive things: they convulse with laughter, with weeping, with orgasms. Somas are the kind of living, organic being which you are at *this* moment, in *this* place where you are. Soma is everything that is you, pulsing within your fragile, changing, growing, and dying membrane that has been chopped off from the umbilical cord which linked you- until the moment of that severance- with millions of years of organic genetic history within this cosmos. The umbilical cord has been severed, and now you stand separated from the umbilical chain, a unique bag of living bone and muscle and nervous tissue and blood- a collection of structured, breathing offal that is somehow you. Somas are you and I, separated without asking from the warm, protective, ever beloved bodies of our mothers, feeling a little alone and a

little confused, wondering what it is all
about, this sixty or seventy years of
pulsing physiological autonomy that was
given without asking and will be taken
away without asking (Hanna, 1970, p.
35).

I like the term soma, and can certainly see
the value in using a fresh word to encourage a
fresh perspective, yet throughout this book I have
chosen to stick with the word *body*. Since body is
the word that English-speakers most often use to
speak of this "bag of living bone and muscle," it
feels important to me to reclaim it from
reductionist thinking by encouraging a more
holistic understanding of it. I am also interested in
the linguistic flexibility of the word, how it is
used to describe larger complex phenomena:
celestial bodies, collective bodies, bodies of
thought, everybody and nobody. I do use the
term somatics though, as a way to ground this
work and research within the lineage of somatic
thinkers who have influenced my own mind and
body.

There is so much more to say about how,
why, and from where this field emerged. If you
are interested, I suggest looking into the history of
the Esalen Institute in Big Sur, California. During
the 1960s and 70s, Esalen was a hub of intellectual

and spiritual experimentation that centered around the mind-body connection and helped inspire many of the modalities that are now generally referred to as somatics. Yet for now, I am going to shift our attention to the various forces that shape bodies and worlds.

CHAPTER 2

Position, Posture, and Point of View:
How Bodies Shape Beliefs

Perspective

"My point of view is first of all literally a viewpoint, my particular angle on life, derived from where and how I stand, reflecting my peculiar leanings and those biases tipping my scale toward one kind of behavior rather than another."

-Don Johnson, *Body* (1983, p. 51)

I recently visited New York City where I was lucky enough to see my first Broadway performance. I'm not typically interested in musicals, nor can I typically afford a Broadway show, but I was willing to make an exception for *Fun Home*. *Fun Home* is based on the life and work of Alison Bechdel, a lesbian comic artist who has a gift for telling stories that are equally heartbreaking and inspiring. This dual appeal of her work is evident even in the title *Fun Home*, which is what she called the funeral home where her family lived and worked.

The story is about differing worldviews and perspectives, and how tragic these differences can be. It's about Alison coming of age and coming out as gay. And

36

it's about her father's suicide, which took place shortly after she came out, and shortly after she found out that her father was also gay. *Fun Home* is essentially an autobiographical reflection of the very home that shaped Alison's experience of life. The beauty of a musical is that it sets the stage for understanding the subtleties and complexities of a story like hers. With great precision and genius, she explains how her childhood home was a reflection of her father's worldview. He occupied the majority of his time and attention toward keeping the house tidy, neat, and polished, protecting the image while in many ways neglecting the family inside.

The scene that really put things into perspective was when Alison, a budding teenager and aspiring graphic artist, was interrupted by her father while she was drawing a comic. A comic is of course made of panels, of small sequenced representation of intimate scenes. Yet to Alison's father, this was a messy and improper technique that lacked focus. Alison's father attempted to explain to her that it's necessary to pick something specific- like a mountain- and draw it with great attention to the big picture, not all the messy details. Alison protested by explaining that a drawing of a mountain- or of a room full of people, or of an entire continent- *is* picking something; it's just a matter of perspective as to what you focus your attention on. Alison's father worked endlessly to protect the big picture image, seemingly unable to accept and attend to the messy details of his inner thoughts and emotional stirrings.

~~~~~~

What I'm proposing is that our particular ideological leanings manifest in our bodies as physical leanings- as the tug and pull that literally shape our musculature through repeated action over time. Alison's worldview, her father's worldview, and the worldview that you and I believe in is a result of perspective, shaped by the places, experiences, and the very bodily angles that we view the world from.

So many words and phrases that are used to describe ideologies and emotions originate from words or phrases that are somatic in nature. For example, the word attitude comes from a 17th century word that meant "a posture of the body to imply some mental state." To be *biased* or *prone* toward something, stems from the Latin *propendere,* meaning "hang forward, hang down, weigh over" (Harper, 2016). We speak about taking a "stance" or a "position" on an issue. We use phrases such as "keep your chin up" to encourage positive thinking. We refer to a stressful situation as a "weight on our shoulders." We describe someone with integrity as being "upright" and a failure or mistake as a "fall." I could go on and on, but the point is that somatic thinking is imbedded in our language. It's something that we are all at least subliminally aware of.

Orientation

What are the factors that determine our "angle" on life? What is it that pulls us and repels us toward and away from objects? Throughout this book I attempt to answer this question in multiple ways, from multiple angles. I began in chapter one by directing our attention briefly toward neuroscience and trauma studies. Understanding the biophysical process that orchestrates our bodily reactions is indeed helpful, but for a moment I want to shift this discussion outside the skin, toward the relational and material environment. By re-directing our attention in this way I am not suggesting that the body and the outside environment are two separate worlds, but I instead want to show how our bodies *extend into* the outside world. This is a question of psychology just as much as it is a question of biology. Yet it moves beyond the realm of both in order to merge the two. One of the first psychologists to propose this merger was Wilhelm Reich (whom I will write about in more detail later). He was attempting to discover this "material force" outside of bodies that pulls us toward or pushes us away from each other.

In looking for my own answer to this question I have found great help and insight from phenomenology. The claim of phenomenology is that consciousness is about perception; it is actively directed toward something. To be conscious of something is to be aware of it, to perceive it.

In other words, consciousness begins when we become conscious of our surroundings.

But what causes us to perceive something? Sara Ahmed, author *of Queer Phenomenology,* has some wonderful insights to offer here. In order to perceive something, we have to see it, or feel it, or sense it. But in order to do so, we have to be oriented toward the object we perceive in the first place. The world is made up of various objects- people, animals, nature, buildings, machines, etc. Some things make impressions on us. We notice them. Some things don't make impressions on us, so we don't notice them. "Orientations involve directions toward objects that affect what we do, and how we inhabit space. We move toward and away from objects depending on how we are moved by them" (Ahmed, 2006, p. 28).

Certain people, places, and objects make impressions on us; they *move* us. Here again, language is an indicator of a somatic phenomenon. We are moved by what moves us. This is an emotional *stirring* that determines if and how we will orient ourselves toward or away from the objects of our affection or dislike. This *movement* determines how we occupy space and how space occupies our attention. As Ahmed explains:

"It is not just that consciousness is directed toward objects, but also that I take different directions toward objects: I might like them, hate them, and so on. In perceiving them in this way or that, I also take a position upon them, *which in turn gives me a position*" (Ahmed, 2006, p. 27).

Early in his career, Thomas Hanna wrote about what he called the *facing function* as "the active way in which the soma moves across the field of universal gravitation toward its intention" (1976). This is contrasted by the somatic function of *backing*, or moving away from an object. It's important to note that moving toward something is not merely directional, but is characterized by what Hanna calls a "somatic appetite." Our attention is *drawn toward* so our bodies *move toward.*

Being oriented toward something is another way of saying that we are facing that object. Yet by facing some things we are ignoring others. According to Thomas Hanna, "awareness is a somatic activity that is exclusive" in that bodies use motor inhibition to exclude sensory information other than what is being focused on (Hanna, 1986).

I don't know about you, but when I begin my day by scrolling through my Facebook feed, I feel disoriented. Usually my intention is to orient myself to what's going on in the world, but if I'm honest, I know I am instead becoming disoriented by algorithms and an overload of opinions.

It's increasingly difficult to stay oriented to our present realities when virtual realities are spewing information at the high-speed of ever-quickening internet connections, disconnecting us from the world in front of us and orienting us away from the present moment.

Also, as we walk through the world, the constant and overwhelming amount of stimuli that characterizes most urban areas require our brains and bodies to decide what to be oriented towards and what to relegate to the background. So much begs for our attention, attempting to move us toward it. The flashy signs of business are designed to draw us in. Traffic signals direct our bodies one way or the other. They tell us to hurry or to wait. When walking through crowded areas, the speed and direction of other walkers invite our bodies to go with the flow. Decisions are made, possibly without noticing, about who to walk around and who to walk over, who to walk towards and who to avoid. A prominent philosopher of phenomenology, Merleau-Ponty, put it beautifully by saying that the body "implies itself to space like a hand to an instrument" (1964, p. 5).

If I'm walking through the woods searching for berries, my attention is directed towards berry bushes. If I am walking through the city looking for ice cream, my attention is directed towards storefronts and street vendors that might sell ice cream. This is my orientation in that moment and it may shift with my shifting desires.

Yet some orientations are more fixed. They are deeply ingrained preferences or biases that bend us in corresponding directions. Sexual orientation, for example, indicates what bodies we tend to be oriented towards as we navigate public space. This isn't to say that we are only oriented towards those we find attractive; it's just one example of an orientation that often has a strong pull.

As another example, I've noticed that as I move through the world I tend to gravitate toward those who have similar interests. If I enter a coffee shop or other social space, I immediately notice the other punks, musicians, or artists. Also, I tend to feel more comfortable around women, so I gravitate toward femme-presenting folks. I am not necessarily making these analytical determinations as I walk into a public space, but somehow still, these factors greatly influence who I face and move towards, and who I ignore.

This is the kind of realization that gives me pause. Does it really serve me to "naturally" orient myself towards those who are most similar to me? Is this some sort of primitive evolutionary drive to find a safe community or tribe? Or is it mostly a divisive function that causes me to ignore those who I can't readily categorize as relatable?

Try to notice this for yourself next time you are in a crowd. What, or who, is drawing you in? What, or who, are you not noticing? Is there anything or anyone you are actively avoiding? Notice what it feels like to avoid. Do you cringe a bit? Does your breath shorten? What would it feel like to move toward someone you'd normally avoid? Do you feel anxious, confident, and/or ambivalent? These feelings are indicators of how we are being pushed and pulled by external forces, yet these forces don't have to control us. Through awareness and practice, we can learn to regain control of our involuntary bodily reactions. I will write at length about this in the final chapter.

We are moved by what moves us. This means that our appetite toward an object, or that, which repels us back, is not always a conscious choice. Without an awareness of how we are being moved by objects, they have a power over us. We are reacting- meaning that there is something outside of us that is causing us to act. Responding is a conscious choice; reacting is a loss of choice, a loss of power. "Turning toward an object turns 'me' in this way or that, even if that turn does not involve a conscious act of interpretation or judgment" (Ahmed, 2006, p. 28).

If our perception of the world is largely determined by what we are oriented towards, and if what we are oriented towards determines what we are oriented *away from*, then it makes sense to take a critical look at what is being missed.

Ahmed observes that so much phenomenological pondering takes place from the "writing table." As phenomenology is concerned with observation, many philosophers begin by observing their immediate environment: the table they are writing from and the room in which the table resides. This is the place that Edmund Husserl, the principal founder of phenomenology, described as "the natural standpoint" from which he viewed the rest of the world. But what is being relegated to the background in order to focus on the table, and on the writing of philosophy in general?

> Ahmed makes a keen observation: We can draw here on the long history of feminist scholarship about the politics of housework: about the way in which women, as wives and servants, do the work required to keep such spaces available for men to do the work they do… To sustain an orientation toward the writing table might depend on such work, while it erases signs of that work… What is behind Husserl's back, what he does not face, might be the back of the house- the feminine space dedicated to the work of care, cleaning, and reproduction. (2006, p. 31)

The writing table is Husserl's point of view. It is the "natural standpoint" from which he views the world. Yet his perception of the world is effected by what he doesn't see. To be invisible means to be relegated to the background, to be unseen, unrecognized. Husserl described reality as he saw it, and this reality did not include what he was not oriented towards. In this way, Husserl's point of view became his worldview. Sara Ahmed suggests that a queer phenomenology might be one that "faces the back," that "looks behind phenomenology" to see what is going unnoticed (Ahmed, 2006). In other words, *to queer* phenomenology would mean to critique this "natural standpoint" as a privileged position, and instead listen to the voices that have been regulated to the background.

As I write this chapter in December of 2016, there is a major historical event taking place at the Standing Rock Native American Reservation. Thousands of indigenous folks and their allies have mobilized from all around the country to converge at the sight of a proposed oil pipeline that would potentially threaten the water supply and health of the land and people who live there, as well as those who live down river. Protests and direct actions have been taking place for months now. It is, to my knowledge, one of the biggest uprisings of Native Americans in decades. Last I heard, over a hundred armed military have arrived on the scene to suppress their efforts. But despite the historical significance of this unprecedented Native uprising, the media has almost entirely ignored the news. Independent journalists who have attempted to report on the events are being shot at with rubber bullets and arrested. Google and Facebook have both been accused of censoring news about the event. Why?

As I have been pondering this question myself and discussing it with friends, I've been reminded of orientation. If the Native American community is familiar with anything, it's familiar with not being seen. One core narrative of the United States is based on a gross misrepresentation and erasure of indigenous struggle and genocide. The indigenous peoples of this land have *violently* been relegated to the background in order for Americans to be oriented towards ownership of this land, to see it as "homeland." It's no surprise that such an orientation is still greatly effecting whether or not we notice or ignore this current struggle.

What I'm beginning to tease out here is how orientation can be both ideological and directional. As I shift between the metaphorical and the material, I am hoping to strip out this dualism. Ideological orientations play out in our bodies by how we show up in the world- which stances we take, who and what we pay attention to, and how we position ourselves around others.

When I was a fundamentalist Christian, my orientation was two-directional: upward, in a kind of hopeful longing towards an infinite sky, and downward, on my knees in repentance. This orientation involved a relegation of my immediate experience. By orienting upwards or downwards, I was neglecting what was in front of me: a direct and curious experience of the world. My head was either in the clouds or in the sand, caught in a hope of the future or a regret of the past, but never in allowance or appreciation of the present. The desire to transcend this world in favor of the next manifested in me as a kind of dissociation noticeable to my peers. I was not oriented towards reality.

I fear (perhaps because I have learned to fear) that my words will not capture the felt experience of this period of my life. This talk of orientation is not an abstraction for the sake of making a point. I was literally so consumed with guilt and so distracted by the "hope of glory" that I had a really difficult time functioning in this world. I wasn't living in this world. I was taught that this world was an evil distraction. As I mentioned in the preface, I was put on medication to help me live in this world. But it didn't work because the problem was not in my brain, *the problem was that my whole body had been inculcated with and shaped by an ideology that orientated me away from this world.*

Alison Bechdel's father took a very specific orientation toward the world as well. His denial of his own sexual orientation caused a tragic disorientation to overtake him. He viewed the world as fixed, which I imagine caused him to see himself as broken. The way Alison tells the story, it makes me think that he was unwilling to adjust his lens to truly capture his experience of life. Perhaps he was unable to accept the complicated and conflicting details of his inner world, letting an innocent longing become a maddening inner turmoil. Closed off and protected, he must have known that facing the longing of his inner world would introduce turmoil to his outer world. How much work it must have taken to keep his world and his house in place, tidy, and organized, despite everything inside of him constantly contradicting itself.

Intention

Somatics is about increasing choice. We have a choice about what we are oriented towards. Richard Strozzi-Heckler, a somatic coach and teacher whose work has greatly influenced me, has proposed that facing can be a *practice*. Our orientation doesn't have to be based solely on what pulls us and what doesn't. Instead, by shifting our awareness, we can make a conscious choice to be oriented toward what is important to us. We can choose to override the reactionary drive away from uncomfortable situations, and instead chose to face the challenges of our life.

Instead of letting our orientation be prescribed by our worldview, or by our fears, we can choose to see things differently. Yet since we are conditioned to see things a certain way, from certain angles, it takes practice to change our point of view.

Strozzi-Heckler proposes that facing with intention is the only way to really see what is in front of us. Facing is not only an acknowledgement of the object or person who is being seen, but also a way of connecting with authenticity. Facing, in this sense, is more than directional; it's about truly seeing. It's the eyes filled with life, it's the sincerity in the hug. It's about being present in an embodied way. It's facing with the whole body, and it's facing with more than just the body.

"When we truly align and face, we see who's there, not just our idea of who we think should be there, or how they should be, or a socially constructed idea of someone, but the person who is actually in front of us" (Strozzi-Heckler, 2007).

In early 2016, I went to a workshop led by a somatic psychologist named Paul Linn, whom I have a lot of respect and admiration for. I showed up with an eager heart, ready to learn, and ready to discover secrets hidden within my own body.

50

On the second day, as we had just warmed up to each other, Paul led us through an intentional practice of facing. We were asked to pick a partner, and face them for several minutes, eyes open. We sat on soft cushions, as stillness entranced the room, and we stared into each other's eyes for what felt like an eternity. It's hard to describe the sensations that filled my body, the love and sincerity that I felt extending toward me, and extending from me. It was profound. I was filled with an uncomfortable nervous energy, an uncontainable giddiness that burst out as laughter and tugged the corners of my lips up into a smile that I couldn't hide, and a smile that was immediately contagious.

At the end of the exercise we hugged, as if saying hello for the first time. We had briefly met, but we both knew that we hadn't really met before that moment. The connection that was formed in that simple gesture of facing, of making contact with our eyes and heart, for just a few minutes, was enough to create a lifelong bond. It was enough to break down walls. I felt seen and I saw.

> When we extend our attention toward someone we become informed about who that person is in the world- his or her attributes, motivations, intention,

and qualities of being. When our conscious attention touches someone and informs our perceptions, there's a dynamic interplay, a reciprocal encounter between the perceiver and the perceived. Extending in this manner is both touching and being touched. It makes us part of who we're communicating with. We touch someone with our attention and they feel touched by it, and touching them touches us. In other words, perception at this level is not a logical calculation but a gregarious participation in the world in which our imagination lends itself to making meaning and direction (Strozzi-Heckler, 2007, p. 148).

~~~~~

As we combat disorientation in the information age, practices that promote stillness and awareness of the present moment will be incredibly helpful. It's a chilling prospect, but it seems that even simply giving ourselves the space to think our own thoughts is becoming a radical act. I have made a commitment to myself to *practice boredom*, which disturbingly seems to be a concept that is disappearing from the human consciousness like a forgotten fad.

Throughout this chapter, I have been attempting to demonstrate how our particular social, ideological, and physical positioning effects how we see the world, how our vantage point becomes our point of view. My especially sensitive nervous system, the particular way that my weight lands on my feet, and the way my pelvis is tilted, all give me a unique outlook on life. In the next chapter, I will begin to unpack some of the ways in which these personal postures and positions can be the result of life experiences and inherited beliefs. Somatics give me hope that a widening posture can result in a widening understanding of the world and of each other. Don Johnson says it well:

> The fear that shapes our flesh… situates us within an enclosed region from which it is difficult to realize that what we see from here is so little of what is… A point of view is healing when it gives a panorama spacious enough to make it obvious that my particular location gives access only to a limited region; without information from people situated on those far distant mountains, valleys and coasts, I and those near to me are condemned to make sense of life with the merest fragments of truth. (1994, p. 5)

CHAPTER 3

Culture and Conditioning:
How Beliefs Shape Bodies

Impulses and Imprints

The American Heritage dictionary describes an *impulse* as "an impelling force, an abrupt inclination." It's the force that causes my heart to jump when I unexpectedly see my partner in the distance. It's the heightened excitement in my voice when a boring conversation turns interesting. It's what Jack Keuroac describes as "visionary tics shimmering in the chest." It's the ideas that have to be spoken aloud, the words that have to get written down. It's that extra energy that comes out of nowhere on the last leg of a marathon.

Merriam-Webster defines *impulse* as "a wave of excitation transmitted through tissues, nerve fibers and muscles." As I have said before, our bodies are not static. We are vibrant living systems that organize in response to our surroundings, our desires, our fears, etc. We experience bodily impulses that pull us towards things we love. We avoid experiences, places, and people that make us feel uncomfortable or unsafe.

My experience of my own body has been shaped by the worldview that was handed to me as a child. I learned to restrict natural impulses that were considered sinful by the teaching of my church. I was taught that all humans are inherently flawed and in need of continual forgiveness. I felt the confusion, doubt, and insecurity of this teaching in my body as an internal sense of guilt, a constant inward reflection and criticism, greatly restricting my outward expression for fear of "acting out" inappropriately. As Don Johnson, a former Jesuit priest and founder of the first graduate program in somatic psychology so bluntly points out in his book *Body*, "My hand is not just the reality outlined in an atlas of anatomy; it is also that which I must keep away from my genitals if I am to avoid hell" (Johnson, 1983, p. 56).

In chapter 2 I began to explore how the stories that we tell ourselves and the stories that we are told about ourselves shape our perspective on life. In this chapter I want to show how these stories also shape the way we *respond* to life. If my experience as a child was that whenever I reached out, whether literally and figuratively, I was ignored, then at some point I probably *learned* to stop reaching out. Not only does this create a psychological barrier that may hinder my ability to ask for help, but it also establishes a flaccidity, or lack of charge, in the arm muscles that are associated with reaching (Macnaughton, 2004). The narratives we absorb, especially early in life, soak deep into our musculature and have real effects on the way we are able to respond to the world.

Lisbeth Marcher, a Scandinavian developmental psychologist, has spent the last 30 plus years of her career testing the theory that the sensory-motor system develops in sync with the psyche. In other words, as certain muscles are being activated for the first time (as we learn to stand, walk, point, etc.) the dynamics of our immediate environment have an effect on the development process. Muscles grow as we age, but which muscles grow rigid and over developed, and which lack vitality, is different for everyone, and is a direct result of how we experience the world.

For example, if a person has difficulty "grasping" or "taking hold" of a situation, a developmental somatic psychologist may look to the muscles of the hands and fingers for insight. The client may be asked to practice grasping. This practice engages the motor function of the hand muscles and strengthens one's ability to grasp onto life. Once again, somatics becomes a matter of semantics. It's not that such a person would lack the motor skills to literally grasp, but that these muscles may lack charge because of information that was imprinted early on. Perhaps every time this client picked up his favorite toy as a child, his caretaker immediately snatched it out of his hand. He may have learned psychologically, as well as muscularly, that there is "no point in trying" to grasp onto the toy (Marcher, 2010, p. 235). By exploring this particular region of the body, it is possible that the associated *somatic memory* may rise to consciousness (see chapter 1) giving the client and therapist further insights to explore.

Bodynamic Institute, the research team that is leading the way in developmental somatic psychology, theorizes that disturbances in the developmental process of motor functions can take place in either the early or late stages of development for each function. Disturbances that take place early on tend to cause a flaccidity of the musculature (as I described in the above example about grasping), while disturbances that take place later in a particular developmental stage tend to cause an excess charge, a rigidity that can result in over-development. In this later stage, once a muscle has already developed a charge, any disturbance is likely to be felt as a challenge or a threat. In response, the muscles develop a rigid defensiveness to protect the agency of the child.

For instance, if the child from my previous example hadn't experienced a disturbance while grasping their toy for a year or so, and then suddenly the care-taker decided that this toy is not to be played with anymore, the child may learn to hold on extra tightly to the toy whenever the caretaker approaches, grasping it for dear life. The muscles learn to latch on and not let go when a threat is perceived. This information gets stored in the body as a learned defense mechanism. It's quite brilliant really; this mechanism serves the child well in that moment, and perhaps also in future situations. Yet it's easy to imagine how this learned pattern could eventually become problematic.

I am aware that it sounds simplistic to blame an overarching psychological disturbance on one's inability to effectively use the muscles of the hand, but I would urge you to consider it for just a moment. Find an object near you and grasp it firmly. What does it feel like? What's changing in your own psychobiology as you squeeze? Do you feel your muscles charging? Do you feel your energy changing? What is your mood?

Why do we urge people to "just hold on" through a difficult moment in life? Why do people judge each other by the firmness of their handshakes? Why is a limp wrist considered effeminate? Why is a clenched fist the symbol of political rebellion? I use these examples not only to show the psychological associations of the "grasping function," but also to highlight how many cultural narratives are wrapped up in this particular gesture.

A seemingly insignificant event like a toy being taken away becomes significant if it is constantly repeated, if it becomes the child's *experience of life*. It is repetition that solidifies and reinforces the narrative that "there's no point." Though a single traumatic event can certainly be the main cause of emotional distress, accumulation of small instances like the one described above can also make a lasting and profound impression. Somatic developmental psychologist and co-founder of the *Bodynamic Institute*, Marianne Bentzen says it well in her article *Shapes of Experience*:

Specific traumatic events are perhaps the most commonly considered reason for personality problems. However, according to developmental research, it is primarily the millions of micro-interactions, beginning before birth and continuing throughout life, that create the very experience of our being in the world. (Marlock, 2015)

Repetition and Repression

When something is repeated, and goes repeatedly unquestioned, it becomes "just the way things are." Why does war exist? Why are some people rich and others poor? Why do I have to work so much just to survive? The answer, so unsatisfactory, often tends to ignore any complex interrogation: "it's just the way things are."

I'm proposing that it's the repetition of experiences that cause them to be seen as "normal." According to queer theorist Judith Butler, as well as a handful of other social theorists, repetition is how dominant narratives take hold. Butler has proposed that social norms such as the nuclear family, heterosexuality, capitalism, etc., become normalized and take "material form" through this effect of repetition (Butler, 1993). Social ideologies solidify to become social structures. When everyone is acting in a way that is congruent with a particular norm, it's hard to see beyond it. It requires a radical shift in perspective to disrupt the cycle of repetition.

I've always been the kind of person to question things. This tendency has been my salvation as well as a constant thorn in my side. I can remember so many instances when I thought of myself as a lunatic or a freak, as the *only one* who didn't think the way everyone else did. It wasn't until I found the other freaks, the other cultural critics, that I realized I wasn't' alone, and that I wasn't crazy. I distinctly remember the moment in my early college experience when I first read Kierkegaard's *The Crowd is Untruth*. Like a lover calming my fears, it spoke sweet words of affirmation to my insecure soul.

Why would anyone question the normalcy of something so solidly configured unless they don't fit into the narrative? Often it's up to these outcasts, the folks on the margins, those who have been relegated to the background, to interrupt a narrative that has been solidified through the power of repetition. I suppose we have these daring rebels to thank for creating the disciplines that have begun to tear down the structures of modernity. Darwin's theory of evolution helped spawn a post-Christian era. Michael Foucault's *History of Madness* called into question the whole paradigm of Western culture. Critical theory, queer theory, and quantum theory are redefining the concept of knowledge itself. It seems to me that even the idea of normalcy has slowly been breaking down.

One of these rebels who threw a wrench into the spokes of Western culture was the complicated and controversial figure Wilhelm Reich. He was a radical psychologist and the person who coined the term "sexual revolution." Reich was a proponent of Karl Marx and a prominent figure of the Freudian left, a contingency of politically-minded psychoanalysts. Reich's career was wedged into a particularly wild nook of human history: right after Freud's ideas of the "unconscious" gained popularity, and right as Hitler was rising to power with his hypocritical and hypnotic hold on the German consciousness. As an Austrian, Reich found himself using his psychoanalytic practice to explore and uncover what he saw as the hidden causes and symptoms of fascism.

Though Reich agreed with Marx's analysis that society's ills were a result of exploitative economic conditions, he was convinced that there was also something deeper going on. He claimed that society affects people in two ways: "directly through the immediate influence of one's economic and social position, and indirectly by means of the ideological structure of society" (1933, p. 18). He was concerned with how morality, such as through the dominant ideas Judeo-Christian theology, can become so deeply imbedded into one's consciousness that it overrides basic survival impulses. "What has to be explained is not the fact that the man who is hungry steals or the fact that the man who is exploited strikes, but why the majority of those who are hungry don't steal and why the majority of those who are exploited don't strike" (1933, p. 19).

During the period of time that Reich was asking these questions, he was also seeing clients in private practice. He began to notice that certain bodily qualities appeared to have rather universal relationships to certain psychological qualities. For example, when a client was depressed and lacking confidence, they would appear to be "deflated" physically, chest sunk, often unable to speak loudly or make eye contact. There was some essential life force missing. This was in stark contrast with the client who exhibited the opposite body: chest puffed out, inflated like a balloon, a stern and towering voice expressing their frustration and anger with all those "under" them. Reich began to realize that the physical manifestation of the body plays a major role in how we experience the world and also limits how we are able to experience the world.

The problem isn't simply that these physical manifestations go unnoticed; it's that people tend to assume that these qualities are simply indicative of their personality. "I'm just not the kind of person who can speak up," or "I've never had much confidence." Yet as Reich began to discover, it is the repetition of these practices (not speaking up) over time that begin to lock these bodily patterns into place.

Reich had a keen eye for how the body is involved in the process of repression. He called for a radical regulation of somatic impulses. Much of his writing began to encompass a critique of the patriarchal family, compulsive morality, and sexual repression. His work with clients began to look very different than Freudian psychoanalysis and he was eventually excommunicated from the fold. By working directly with people's bodies, he attempted to access memories and sensations that had been blocked by the tensing of muscles. Instead of viewing his clients as diseased or mentally unstable, he implicated the repressive ideologies of society as the cause of people's inability to express or access their natural impulses and desires.

For example, if an exploited worker wants to speak up to her boss, but instead tends to habitually clench her jaw to hold back her frustration, this causes the musculature of the throat to get locked into a contraction state. What was at first the body's way of helping her to hold her tongue then becomes a muscular contraction that also inhibits her ability to speak up in the future. This then becomes "just the way she is" or in Reich's terms it becomes part of her "character structure."

Alexander Lowen, a student of Reich who became instrumental in forwarding Reich's ideas, said it like this: "The suppression of impulses is not a conscious or selective process like the act of holding back their expression. It is the result of the continual holding back of expression until that holding back becomes a habitual mode and an unconscious body attitude" (Lowen, 1972, p. 81).

Bodies take the shape of what they repeatedly do. Reich noticed that in people who primarily tense the muscles of one area of the body, that area tends to develop noticeably larger and with more rigid muscular tension than in other areas. This observation was so consistent across the board that Reich developed a whole system of psychoanalysis based on these patterns of muscular holding. He theorized that these muscular patterns indicate blocked impulses (or holding patterns) and in turn can predict behavior patterns. This theory is laid out in his classic 1933 book *Character Analysis.* Somatic psychology as a field has since become less prescriptive. Practitioners tend not to work from such a rigid vantage point of characterizing and categorizing. But that being said, Reich's ideas and formulations have been unequivocally foundational to the field and its development.

Sadly, the world wasn't ready for Wilhelm Reich's radical ideas. He died in a United States prison shortly after being arrested for running experiments and selling equipment that defied the regulations of the then extremely powerful Federal Department of Agriculture. The government burned his books, and his reputation. Luckily, some of the copies escaped the incinerator and his books have since been reprinted. It wasn't until years later that Reich's legacy would emerge to reveal the powerful visionary he was. When the "sexual revolution" actually arrived in the spring of 1968, students in Berlin hurled copies of Reich's *Mass Psychology of Fascism* at the police. In

Paris, Reich's notorious symbol of sexual freedom was graffitied on walls of the Sorbonne (Elking, 1971).

~~~~~~

It's not easy to break the cycle of repetition, to interrupt a narrative that has become normalized through years, or even centuries, of consistency. It takes courage and the strength to navigates one's own shame in order to speak out. As my previous example of an exploited worker shows, such hesitancy often involves a fear that has taken "material form" as muscular constriction of the throat. To complicate things even further, one may not simply be challenging an idea, but an entire *structure* of society that has been solidified and institutionalized through years of repetition.

I once heard an enlightening story about a Buddhist monastery. In their beginning years, a neighborhood cat would frequently wander into the monastery and sit next to the statue of the Buddha. One week, a member of the group placed a little hat on the cat and everyone laughed. From then on it became a running joke. Every time the cat would enter the monastery, the same little hat would be placed on its head. Decades passed and membership of the monastery shifted, yet the tradition of placing the hat on the cat continued. The cat became seen as a meaningful spiritual figure to the members of the monastery. Eventually it became such an important ritual that the gatherings could not begin until the cat, and the hat, were in place. Whenever a new member asked why this happened, they were given a pious answer about the sanctity of the cat and the importance of the ritual. Yet no one actually knew why it started, or why it was still happening. It just became the way things are.

This is a silly example. But how much less silly is it to place a cookie on the counter for an imaginary Santa Claus to eat? Or the ritual of a priest turning grape juice into the blood of Christ and drinking it? A ritual is born when meaning is ascribed to an otherwise meaningless act. The meaning becomes encoded and solidified through repetition.

To me, rituals can be a beautiful and significant part of being human. They connect to our stories and our ancestors. They ground us in the present and allow us to remember the past in a way that is often somatically and spiritually rich. Unfortunately, over time the original meaning often gets muddied and obscured, replacing its richness with an uncharitable sense of obligation.

Once a narrative has been repeated with enough frequency, it often becomes part of the social fabric. Social norms and structures become invested in upholding it, sometimes even to the degree that a partial deviation from the dominant narrative becomes seen as a threat to the entire fabric of society. As the Religious Right campaigns against gay marriage, they warn of the entire *concept of love and family* being under threat.

According to the most dominant narratives, including the religious ones, the way things are *is the way things have always been*. From this perspective, from this moral position, change is seen as an unraveling of the universe, or of God's plan, or of reality- whichever divine force is assumed to be responsible. When a social norm becomes linked to morality, it's impact on bodies often involves a felt sense of shame and guilt. Muscles learn to harden against impulses that contradict the accepted moral system.

In my view, and judging from my own experience, it seems that a narrative has a stronger grasp on bodies if it is tied to a moral system. Shame and guilt keeps one's perspective narrow by forbidding inquisitive thought. Though I think that this is an intentional technique of conditioning that is rooted in the preservation of the narrative, I also think that it can be equally unintentional. The complicated thing about religious forms of abuse, for example, whether we are talking about cults or trauma-inducing belief systems, is that often the people who are doing the manipulating are also manipulated.

I don't hold grudges for the things I was taught to believe as a child. Of course I feel angry sometimes, especially knowing that so many are currently being forced to believe in the same demons that haunted me. Yet still, I don't see it as an intentional attack on vulnerable minds, but instead as a cycle that has been repeated for so long that it's almost impossible for those caught up in it to see beyond it. This is why I'm not throwing bricks at the cathedral. Instead I'm focused on deconstructing the pieces of the narrative that have been harmful to me, dismantling the emotional blocks in own my body that keep me from experiencing a fullness of life, and offering this work as a tool to others who feel trapped in any sort of constricting narrative.

~~~~~

Cultural conditioning is a bodily phenomenon. The developmental psychologist Lev Vygotsky put it this way, "Every function in cultural development appears twice: first, on the social level, and later, on the individual level; first, between people… and then inside" (1978, p. 57). From a somatics point of view, cultural conditioning and somatic conditioning are one in the same.

Reflecting on Pavlov's experiment with dogs, Thomas Hanna explains, "conditioning is a manipulative technique of forcing an adaptive response on the body's involuntary reflex mechanisms" (Hanna, 1986). Yet as I was attempting to explain above, Hanna points out that conditioning can also happen unintentionally through the repetition of norms:

> The same form of conditioning can also
> take place in uncontrived ways…
> Environmental situations that pose a
> constant stimulus on deep survival
> reflexes will, with sufficient repetitions,

> make them habitual- the reflex becomes
> learned... habituated... there is a dual
> loss of conscious control of that area of
> motor action and conscious sensing of
> that motor action. (1986)

In other words, conditioning, as discussed earlier, involves a process of repetition (of muscular holding, of putting a hat on a cat, of grasping tightly to a ball) that becomes involuntary and unconscious over time. These involuntary actions and unquestioned behavior patterns don't necessarily have to be tied to a grand narrative or traumatic event, they can be the result of years of repeated micro-interactions that have informed one's perspective on life. The learned tendency to "hold on tightly" or perhaps to "never hold on tightly" gets absorbed from the fabric of our social environment into the fabric of our muscular system, shifting from macro to micro.

What we continually do with our bodies as a result of these narratives also works to reinforce them. These learned patterns of behavior become our tendencies. Again, the linguistic roots of the word *tendency* have to do with "movement" and involve a "leaning effect." Formed and molded by learned patterns, impulses and habits, bodies take the shape of what they repeatedly do.

If your body tends to exhibit a forward lean, pushing the majority of your weight onto the front of your feet, it is quite likely that this *bodily tendency* to over-extend is correlated with a *habitual tendency* to over-extend in

69

other ways: over-committing, talking over people, etc. The muscles of the body are naturally and energetically oriented in extension toward the world. Someone who exhibits this bodily quality may have a difficult time holding back.

In the same way, if your body is typically pulled toward the back, pushing your weight onto your heels, it is likely that you have a tendency to hold back in life, to live with a constant hesitancy. This could stem from an early history of rejection. It may also represent a kind of apathy or complacency, keeping you from moving forward. The point it not to diagnose, but to notice. In his book *Narrative Medicine*, Mehl-Madrona explains, "master narratives become habitual to the extent that their enactment becomes our routine... they constrain and delineate our freedom to choose to do otherwise, effectively reducing our range of potential action" (2007). These bodily tendencies can then be indicators of internalized stories. Paying attention to them is the first step in shifting our habits and re-aligning the way we want to act with the way we act.

Throughout this chapter I propose that bodies are shaped by habit and repetition, or more specifically, by the push and pull of our beliefs. Often these beliefs that shape us are the result of patterns that emerge as we learn to regulate impulses and behaviors according to the expectations of culture. In the next chapter I will show

how this imposed somatic regulation often involves unseen forces that are highly political.

CHAPTER 4

The Politics of Expansion and Contraction

What Emotions Do

In chapter one, I defined emotions as an interpretation of bodily sensations. An emotion (fear, sadness, anger) is the name we give to a feeling arising in our bodies. A racing heart, for example, isn't simply a symptom of fear, but is the very thing that we are calling fear. By this definition, fear would cease to exist if the heart was beating slowly. If my heart was beating slowly and someone asked me how I feel, I would say that I feel *calm*. So in this way, emotions are the names we give to bodily sensations. A review of chapter 1 will refresh your memory on this interplay of feelings and emotions.

There are a couple of competing popular theories about what emotions are and where they come from. The view I am working with in this book- emotions as bodily sensations- can be attributed to philosophers such as William James, David Hume, and surprisingly enough, Descartes (Ahmed, 2004). Though Descartes has gained a notoriously negative reputation for initiating the idea of the mind/body split, some of his other ideas actually held the body in high esteem.

The other popular theory of emotions regards them as primarily cognitive. This idea can be traced to Aristotle and tends to be the dominant theory among individualist Western psychologies. In this theory, fear exists because one makes a cognitive judgment that something is to be feared. Simply stated, the emotion "begins" inside a person's brain. The rest of the body doesn't play much of a role in this process, other than maybe getting in the way.

I am no scientist, and I have no stake in answering this question definitively. I think there is room for competing theories to coexist and complement each other. So, instead of diving deeper into the question of what emotions are, I'd like to spend some time in this chapter asking a different question: What do emotions do?

I will mostly be drawing from the ideas that Sara Ahmed put forth in her 2004 book *The Cultural Politics of Emotions*. This book has been foundational to my thinking about bodies. It's been my guiding map in many ways. Reading this book struck an impulse deep inside of me that has been vibrating with curiosity and excitement ever since. For this reason, I am going to spend a good deal of this chapter focusing on Ahmed's work.

She proposes that emotions are always *about something*, meaning that they involve an orientation toward or away from an object. If I am walking in the woods and I see a bear, I may halt in my tracks, and my heart may begin racing. I might freeze and become immobile or my legs may begin mobilizing for flight. This all happens before I make a cognitive calculation about the bear. Before I analyze whether or not I should be afraid, my body is already in a reaction state. The emotion is not just "in my head" but is *directed toward something*. I am reacting to the bear.

When I see the bear, my body makes a judgment. My tightened tissues have decided that the bear is to be feared. So in this sense, emotional reactions involve bodily sensations *and* judgments. Yet the judgments are not necessarily cognitive; they are judgments that our bodies make before cognitive awareness catches up. So where do these judgments of the body come from? In chapter one I cited neuroscientist Antonio Damasio's theory of somatic markers to show that memories and associations from the past become stored in our bodies as information. If I lived with a housemate in the past that I didn't get along with, I may have a "gut feeling" that it's a bad idea to live with that person again. I will continue here with this line of thinking and begin to tease out how these gut feelings or pre-cognitive associations become tied to certain objects in the first place.

Before I continue, I should clarify what I mean by "object." Ahmed and other philosophers use this word to refer to anything, material or otherwise, that a person comes in contact with, or is "involved with." By this definition, an object may refer to a building or to a city, to a person or to a group of people, or even to something more ethereal like an idea, an ideology, or a memory (2004,

p. 7). As I showed in chapter one, ideas and memories can certainly evoke feeling. So anything that a body may come in contact with that has the potential to evoke feeling is an object, in this context.

So why do certain objects evoke certain feelings? How does an object take on an association? I'm proposing that this involves more than just our past experience, but that it is also wrapped up in the narratives we are told, and tell ourselves, about certain objects. Why would the sight of a bear evoke a fear response in a child? Is this response instinctual in an evolutionary sense, or is it because the child has *learned* that bears are to be feared? Ahmed argues for the latter, taking more of a social constructionist stance on emotion.

She suggests that the child has learned that bears are to be feared and this association is triggered in the child's body as a response to the bear. Perhaps this child had a previous encounter with a bear that was traumatic, or maybe her parents had warned her that bears are dangerous. The association of the bear as fearsome is a result of this narrative being repeatedly expressed and internalized. I'm not arguing that this reaction to the bear is invalid or inappropriate, instead I am simply exploring where it came from. Would the knee-jerk reaction of fear and tension still happen if the child was repeatedly told that bears are friendly and harmless? Would the association still be present if the bear in this story was a small cub and not a large grizzly?

It is not that the bear *is* fearsome 'on its own,' as it were. It is fearsome *to* someone or somebody. So fear is not in the child, let alone in the bear, but is a matter of how child and bear come into contact. This contact is shaped by past histories of contact, unavailable in the present, which allows the bear to be apprehended as fearsome. The story does not, despite this, inevitably lead to the same ending. Another child, another bear, and we might have another story. (p. 7)

This example serves its purpose, but to me it's a messy example. It seems too easy to get caught up in the debate about whether fear of bears is an *instinctual* reaction or a *learned* reaction. It's a question that could be debated for a while because not many people would disagree that bears do, and should, evoke fear. Yet what if the main character in this analogy was not a bear, but instead a migrant farmworker from Mexico, or a person of the Muslim faith? As I am writing this, President Elect Donald Trump is spouting messages of fear about how dangerous "illegal immigrants" and Muslims are. I'll ask the same question that I did before: Is this fear response instinctual in an evolutionary sense, or is it because one has learned that Muslims, Immigrants, etc., are to be feared?

What do emotions do? If seeing a person of Arab descent invokes a fear response, then what emotions do, in this case, is keep us apart.

"Fear shapes the surfaces of bodies in relation to objects. Emotions are relational: they involve (re)actions or relations of 'towardness' or 'awayness'" (p. 8).

Citing Descartes, Ahmed explains that "objects do not excite diverse passions because they are diverse, but because of the diverse ways that they may harm or help us" (p. 5). What I believe Descartes is saying here is that objects are not necessarily good or bad, but they evoke a response in us based on whether *we see them* as good or bad, as harmful or helpful. So the "diverse passions" that become "excited" as a result of contact with an object involve an interpretation of whether that object is harmful or helpful, and this interpretation is likely to be the result of what one has learned to believe about the object.

Again, Ahmed proposes that emotions are about something. Sensations arise in bodies as a result of contact with objects. As social beings in a material and relational world, we are in constant contact with objects: the chairs we sit in, the roads we walk down, the people we live with, work with, sleep with. Even seemingly meaningless things such as the cup of coffee sitting on my desk, the empty beer can next to it, and the cat in my living room causing my allergies to flare up, are all examples of the multitude of "objects" that I am in contact with at this moment. And they all hold various associations to me.

Yesterday, on my way home, I passed by a gas station that sparked a memory of a past relationship. A year prior, my ex-partner and I had one of our most difficult and final conversations standing in front of this station. I was immediately overtaken by subtle sensations of regret and sadness as I passed by yesterday. I didn't consciously turn my attention to that memory; it *grabbed* me unexpectedly as a result of coming into contact with an object that held those associations.

What do emotions do? In this case, emotions connected me to the past in a self-reflective way.

Bodies are in constant contact with objects. If objects hold associations that are tied to past memories, and if those associations generate feeling, then bodies are constantly being affected by emotional intensities. It makes total sense that we have learned to block feelings, especially in crowded concrete cities that relentlessly rumble with affect. With constant stimulation, we are constantly feeling, and sometimes feeling everything is just too much.

In the midst of this sensory overload, it can be hard to distinguish between the sensations being evoked. When I passed that gas station the other day, I had time to process the feelings that arose. Yet if I was in a rush, or if I was already distracted, I may not have attended to these feelings. Perhaps after rushing to where ever I was going I would have wondered why I was having random feelings of regret and sadness. I may have had no clue what sparked the feelings in the first place.

Having so much competing for our attention, along with being raised in a culture that ignores feeling, it is easy for emotions and their associations to become "displaced" and get lost in the rush. If we are not consciously paying attention to the sensations and feelings rising in or bodies, it can be easy to lose contact with our sense of self and become anxious, irritable, or otherwise overwhelmed

This is where it becomes essential to make the distinction between feeling and emotion. As I explained in chapter one, feelings enter into our bodies in response to stimuli without us having a choice in the matter- guttural stirrings, sunken hearts, braced muscles. Yet what we do with these feelings, how we respond to them, how we interpret and internalize them is- or at least can be- a matter of choice. For example, if someone throws a football across the park and it accidentally hits me in the face, my nerves will become excited and my body may be thrown into fight mode. Yet if I pause and realize that it was an accident, I can regain a sense of control. In this example, the sudden excitement of my nerves and muscles being mobilized for fight or flight is a bodily *feeling*, and my response of rage, anger, or calmness is the associated *emotion* that gets evoked.

Some people might certainly react to this scenario with rage, raring for a fight. Yet I would bet that what they are reacting to has less to do with the football and more to do with a history of experiences that are being triggered in that moment. As I will explain later in this study, somatic awareness allows for a crucial pause in the moment between stimulation and response. This gives us the opportunity to consider what is truly causing us to feel a certain way, and to determine how and if we will respond instead of simply reacting.

The point I am trying to make, though it may seem counterintuitive, is that opening ourselves to the plethora of life's feelings actually increases our capacity to respond to them. As we become acquainted with our feelings and reactive tendencies, we will gain a deeper understanding of where the thoughts, beliefs, and stories that are being triggered are coming from. As we open our bodies to allow the flow of feeling, we will increase our capacity to let unwanted feelings pass through, diminishing their intensity, instead of letting them become lodged in our musculature.

Another possible reaction is to completely block a certain feeling from entering our body and consciousness. If a feeling is uncomfortable, we may subconsciously tense our muscles to harden against the feelings being evoked. Over time, with enough repetition, this muscular pattern becomes chronic and the emotion gets blocked out of consciousness all together. We stop feeling the emotion, as such, and instead feel the tensing of the muscles that are activated to block the feeling. This may become our habitual reaction to difficult feelings. Yet this muscular rigidity has an emotional quality in and of itself.

> Sara Ahmed reminds us *hardness is not the absence of emotions, but is a different emotional orientation towards others*... We shouldn't look for emotional intensities 'in' soft bodies. Emotions shape the very surfaces of bodies, which take shape through the repetition of actions over time, as well as orientations toward and away from others. (p. 4)

Not only are emotions felt as sensations, but they also cause bodies to do certain things. My stomach might churn, or my lips quiver, or my eyebrows rise. I might quicken my pace or clench my jaw. Our bodies are literally shaped by how we respond to objects and others (turning in, turning away, moving towards, moving away).

As bodies navigate space, certain things pull us in while some things repel us. One might avoid certain people, or certain kinds of people based on one's impressions. I might tear up if I see a person desperately begging for money. Someone else might tense up. I might feel upset and defeated by the onslaught of political advertisements all around me, someone else might feel inspired and compelled towards action. Seeing an image of a bloody Jesus may cause some hearts to expand with love and thankfulness. For me, seeing the same image used to cause my body to tense, my chest to contract and my breath to shorten. If I see the same image now, I feel nothing.

What do emotions do? Emotions give shape to our bodies as we react to the objects around us. Bodies take the shape of what we repeatedly do.

Impressions and Interpretations

Ahmed suggests that the "impressions" that objects make on us are literally impressions: they press against and shape our bodies. They make us cringe or expand, move away or be drawn towards. As I explained in the previous chapter, reactions that are repeated over time become habitual, they become involuntary and unconscious. In this sense, an impression that I have of something, over time, may become my solid belief about that something, and may show up in my body as a habitual reaction towards or away from the object that has made an impression on me. Alexander Lowen writes: An impression is the opposite of an expression. When an impulse affects another person, he receives an impression. The impulse need not be a blow; it may be a look, a gesture or a word. The impression is the result of an external force acting on the body. (1972, p. 79)

In this way, an impression often involves an interpretation of an expression, which all too often can actually be a misinterpretation. Our interpretation of someone's expression is often determined by the history of impressions we already have about that person. Discrimination can exist in the form of bodily reactions.

Let me give an example. A black person and a white person encounter each other on an empty city street. The white person has been watching the nightly news, which routinely describes every "suspicious" character creeping around the neighborhood as "a black male wearing a hoodie." As they near each other the white person subconsciously begins walking faster out of fear. The black person reads this as possible aggression because of past trauma and exhibits a demeanor of defensiveness. The white person reads this defensiveness as aggressiveness and cuts the corner in a hurry, rushing away. This fearful encounter becomes stored in the white person's body as a barely avoided danger, reinforcing the oppressive narrative that black people are dangerous. Though the encounter was based on a misreading of each other's bodies, it affectively re-established the distance between the two. The feeling is remembered by the musculature and stored as a belief about blackness that will inform future encounters. In this way fear works to establish distance between bodies, reinforcing disconnection and often involving a misreading of the other.

Fear also works to keep certain bodies out of certain spaces. The bodily manifestation of fear is a contraction of the musculature, a drawing inward. This keeps unwanted bodies from taking up space. Ahmed says it well: "Fear works to contain bodies within social space through the way it shrinks the body, or constitutes the bodily surface through an expectant withdrawal from a world that might yet present itself as dangerous" (p. 70).

> Drawing from feminism Ahmed points out: Such feelings of vulnerability and fear hence shape women's bodies as well as how those bodies inhabit space. Vulnerability is not an inherent characteristic of women's bodies; rather, it is an effect that works to secure femininity as a delimitation of movement in the public, and over-inhabitance in the private. (p. 70)

The oppressive narrative that a woman's place is in the house contains a flip side: the outside world is too dangerous.

If social spaces are designed for the comfort and ease of dominant groups, then it is only marginalized groups who feel the effects of not "fitting in." Drawing from queer theory and her own lived experiences Ahmed gives the example that "heteronormativity functions as a form of public comfort by allowing bodies to extend into spaces that have already taken their shape." From the images on billboards to the music being played on the radio, social space is shaped to validate and reinforce social norms. She goes on to say, "one does not notice this as a world when one has been shaped by that world and even acquired its shape. Norms… have a way of disappearing from view" (p. 148).

HB2, the recent legislation that passed in North Carolina, provides a timely example. The law restricts transgender people from using the bathrooms that match their gender. Though it is not practical to enforce this law, the fear of potential violence is certainly felt as a material force that presses against the bodies of those who "do not belong." This creates a particularly troubling anomaly for trans folks as fear of violence may be equally felt whether they use the legal restroom (and are perceived as an intruder) or if they use the illegal restroom (and are found out). Additionally, anyone who doesn't comfortably fit into either side of the gender binary is viewed with suspicion and risks violence.

As I suggested in chapter 2, when a person's sexual orientation doesn't match how society is oriented, then it manifests as a kind of disorientation. Ahmed offers a personal context as an example:

> I know this feeling too well, the sense of
> out-of-place-ness and estrangement
> involves an acute awareness of the
> surface of one's body… when one cannot
> inhabit the social skin, which is shaped
> by some bodies and not others.
> Furthermore, queer subjects may also be
> 'asked' not to make heterosexuals feel
> uncomfortable by avoiding the display of

signs of queer intimacy, which is itself an
uncomfortable feeling, a restriction of
what one can do with one's body, and
another's body, in social space. (p. 148)

Feminist scholar Marilyn Frye authored an
excellent essay that gives voice to the effect that oppression
of many forms can have on bodies:

The experience of oppressed people is
that the living of one's life is confined
and shaped by forces and barriers which
are not accidental or occasional and
hence avoidable, but are systematically
related to each other in such a way as to
catch one between and among them and
restrict or penalize motion in any
direction. It is the experience of being
caged in: all avenues, in every direction,
are blocked or booby-trapped. (Frye,
1983)

This discussion of fear is relevant to my own lived
experience of oppressive forces. God became the object of
my fear. The stories that I was told, with all of their
contradictions and misinterpretations (of the bible),
accumulated as an intense anxiety. My impression of God
caused a pressing upon my body that resulted in near
paralysis. The narrative of the world as evil, deceptive, and
full of temptation caused me to shrink inward and away
from it. The intensity of my reaction was multiplied by the

fact that I wasn't moving away from a singular object, but a kind of subjective totality: the world.

Ahmed suggests that the turning away from the object of fear also involves a "turning toward the object of love," as in a child huddling into her mother's arms in the face of a perceived danger. For me, and for so many others, fundamentalist Christianity produced a confused reality in which I viewed God as my oppressor and my savior, the object of my fear and the object of my love. The trinity represents a kind of circulation of contradicting affect: the rigid hard-to-please Father, loving acceptance and forgiveness through the Son, all mediated by the work of the Holy Spirit. Perhaps it was this felt confusion that caused my body to become paralyzed. Like a deer in headlights, I froze in fear.

To be clear, I am not using this as a metaphor. When my anxiety was at its worst, I literally became paralyzed for days at a time. I didn't just repress a few sinful impulses here and there; I literally repressed every impulse. I shut down. I was quite literally traumatized. And I'm sure the cocktail of pharmaceuticals I was ingesting daily didn't help my dissociation.

> The root of the word 'oppression' is the
> element 'press.'…Presses are used to mold
> things or flatten them or reduce them in
> bulk, sometimes to reduce them by
> squeezing out the gases or liquids in them.
> Something pressed is something caught

between or among forces and barriers,
which are so related to each other that
jointly they restrain, restrict or prevent the
thing's motion or mobility. Mold.
Immobilize. Reduce. (Frye, 1983)

An experience of shame may manifest in a sort of
turning away from others and inward towards the self.
This involves a tightening of the fascia and a contraction of
the whole muscular system, which squeezes the organs
and shortens the breath. An experience of love or
connection manifests very differently, as an expansion of
the self and the muscular system causing a literal opening
of the heart.

The word *shame* comes from the Indo-European
verb meaning "to cover" (Ahmed, 2004). There is a sense
of concealment, of wanting to hide, to sink within oneself
and away from the world. Ahmed points out that we often
"feel shame because we have failed to appropriate 'an
ideal' that has been given to us..." She goes on to say that
"this is why shame has been seen as crucial to moral
development; the fear of shame presents the subject from
betraying 'ideals'" (2004, p. 106).

Ahmed explains, "if contact with an object generates
feeling, then emotion and sensation cannot be easily
separated. A common way of describing the relationship
between them is as a form of company: pleasure and pain
become companions of love and hate" (p. 8). So if a
sensation being generated is pleasurable, I may associate it

with love, and be open to it. Floating with a sense of lightness and a charged impulsive energy, my whole body will expand toward the object of my desire.

On the other hand, suppression of desire, oppression and negative impressions about people all have a pressing, contracting, immobilizing effect on the musculature. Impulses toward action, toward expansion, toward love become more difficult to access. The body is locked in a state of contraction. The density of this constriction is felt as a sense of heaviness, as if gravity is too much to bear.

Depression, as you may notice, also involves a pressing effect. The language of the body may be verbally expressed as "feeling down," as if there is a "weight on the shoulders." In his book *Depression and the Body*, Alexander Lowen explains that "we can speak therefore of depression being an internal collapse, meaning that the ability of an organism to respond with appropriate impulses to environmental events has greatly diminished" (1972, p. 79). Lowen also points out that there is a direct correlation between depression and one's ability to take full breathes. Compression of the chest causes one to be unable to inspire fully, and consequently, to be fully inspired.

The human organism is designed to be in a constant state of contraction and expansion. Our lungs, hearts, tissues, and cells are pulsating as we inhale and exhale. Our hearts pump life into our being moment by moment. We grab hold of what we want, and we learn to let go. Each morning our eyes open, and each night they close. This is a healthy state of somatic regulation. When bodies are able to experience this flux and flow, free of constriction, there is a felt sense of vitality and life.

We are bodies that are shaped and molded by our environments, life experiences, worldviews, habits, and personal and cultural histories. Though we are easily malleable we are also incredibly powerful. Our resilience is in our flexibility, our ability to shift shape and shift the narratives that have shaped us. In the next and final chapter, I will begin to explore ways that we can move towards this transformation.

CHAPTER 5

Free, Dynamic, and Just Social Bodies

"We are ideas made of flesh
our goosebumps raise questions we do not ask--
hesitations held
so close to our chest,
tightly...
until we burst."
-Nina Go

Changing the Story

I was in therapy for years trying to relieve the chronic anxiety that was crippling my body. Beginning in middle school, I began a harrowing journey of trying out every counselor, psychologist, psychiatrist and medication that my parents thought could possibly help. None of it worked. I kept hearing over and over, from every therapist, that there was something different about my situation, something they couldn't understand. So they gave up, one by one, and my parents and I began to think that this problem of mine was never going to be resolved.

Yet this "problem of mine," to a huge extent, was that I existed in a problematic paradigm. In my later teenage years I finally saw a therapist who seemed to understand this. She didn't give up on me. She treated me like I was a person with a hard life, not a person with a brain disease. She asked me about my future, my hopes, and my desires. No one had ever done that. Everyone else just went down a checklist with blank stares, holding a clipboard, and tilting their heads in confusion when my answers didn't match their boxes.

This new therapist made subtle suggestions that my anxiety was stemming from the religious ideas I had internalized, but I didn't bite. Presumably in an attempt to remain professional, she didn't push the issue, even though it was as undeniable as the sun blasting through her second story office. This would-be powerful transformative work was halted, at least until later.

When I left my hometown at 20 years old, the world opened up to me. I moved to Gainesville, a small college town in Florida which is a hotspot of punk music, activism, and art. I was exposed to different worldviews, religions, and sexualities. I discovered critical thoery and post-modern authors. My limited narrative was beginning to expand, and as it did I could feel my body expanding. My constricting worldview was losing power and loosening its grip on my rib cage. My anxiety slowly subsided. Impulses towards life were allowed to flow and I felt free to follow them. I fondly remember this period of my life as an extremely liberating and exciting time.

I barely slept. I had awoken to life and I needed to use every moment I had to follow every impulse and curiosity as I re-oriented myself toward a world full of possibility, a world that was no longer evil or dangerous, a world that I had missed out on. I would stay up all night searching the Internet for answers to all my biggest questions. I joined a liberal Christian church that helped me to embrace doubt and complexity, and to heal my hellish thoughts. I read forums and joined online support networks with others who had grown up in fundamentalist environments. I was slowly deconstructing my reality and creating a new one.

This burst of feeling and impulse was the beginning of a powerful and profound somatic transformation that was the immediate result of a shifting personal narrative. Richard Strozzi-Heckler describes this sort of "illuminative quickening" in this way:

> When we feel we find ourselves...
> transported to a more amplified level of
> aliveness... We find ourselves in new
> conversations and responsive to urges
> that previously didn't seem to exist. The
> categories that we are accustomed to are
> no longer relevant and the boundaries
> that are dear to us come in to question;
> they are now more elastic and porous
> than we imagined. (2014, p. 49)

Although I spent years in therapy being analyzed by trained psychologists, none of them (except one) could see beyond the surface. They were oriented towards the prevailing model of cognitive psychology, which, in my case, completely missed what was actually going on. The context that I existed in, the turmoil that was so obviously linked to my beliefs about the world, and the fear that was so potently gripping my body were all ignored by a model of psychology that favors scientific reductionism and individual pathology rather than looking at issues of social and environmental trauma. In hindsight, what I needed was to expand my worldview and to change my environment. And as soon as I did that, I was able to throw away my pills and I literally never experienced a symptom again.

I can't overstate the immediacy of this change. Yes, it took me years to untangle the constricting narrative of fundamentalist Christianity that I had inherited. Yet the moment that I opened myself up to the possibility that hell does not exist, I was a new person. The moment that I learned that the doctrine of eternal punishment, which I had taken as truth, was perhaps instead an extreme misinterpretation of the original text, I felt a catastrophic release, a weight being lifted off of my body, an exorcism of sorts. I saw the world with new eyes, full of vivid colors that I couldn't see before.

~~~~~

In 1989, Ignacio Martin-Baro, head of the psychology department at the University of Central America in San Salvador, wrote a biting critique of Western psychology that has shaped and validated my own understanding of mental health. His work was highly influenced by Paulo Friere's concept of "awakening the critical consciousness," which proposes that societal change will bubble up from the ground if marginalized people become conscious of the oppressive forces that shape them, and are awakened to their own autonomy and power. Martin-Baro spoke out against individualist and cognitive-based psychologies, claiming, "individualism ends up reinforcing the existing structures because it ignores the reality of social structures and reduces all structural problems to personal problems" (1994, p. 22).

The authors of the 2008 book *Toward Psychologies of Liberation* describe Martin-Baro's philosophy in this way:

> [He] understood that 'the healing power of any psychotherapeutic method depends on the dosage of its break with dominant culture, 'which he described as 'the veil of lies we move about in.' In part, the construction of a more just society is 'a mental health concern' requiring us to 'work hard to find theoretical models and methods that

allow us, as a community and as individuals, to break with the culture of vitiated social relations, and put other, more humanizing relations in their place.' His interdependent goals for liberation psychology were 'healthy, free, and creative minds' in a 'free, dynamic, and just social body.' (2008, p. 25)

Martin-Baro predicted that he would be silenced as soon as he published this critique, and sadly, he was. In 1989, the year his *Writings for a Liberation Psychology* was published, he was assassinated by the Atlacatl Battalion, a "counter-insurgency unit" created at the U.S. Army's School of the Americas, presumably as a result of his attempt to raise the political consciousness of the oppressed (Levine, 2014).

Martin-Baro is not the only one that has raised these direct critiques of western psychology. Since its inception, there has been a long lineage of lamenters who see the individualist-orientation of Western psychology to be particularly problematic. The anti-psychiatry movement of the 1960s and 70s is one example, inspired by the ideas of Thomas Szasz, R. D. Laing, and Michel Foucault. The writings of Wilhelm Reich certainly also encapsulated this critique. Judi Chamberlin's 1978 text, *On Our Own: Patient Controlled Alternatives to the Mental Health System,* inspired a movement toward peer-run, trauma-informed, and community-based mental health services. I am currently the program coordinator for one such organization.

In 2003, shortly after I left the fundamentalist bubble of my hometown and moved to Gainesville, FL, I saw an advertisement for the Icarus Project. It read *"What does it mean to be called crazy in a world that is obviously insane?"* An immediate curiosity shot through my body like a drug. Could this be real? Are these my people?

The Icarus Project, now almost 15 years strong, is a support network by and for people who experience the world in a way that, by conventional standards, might be considered abnormal. It's for people like me, people who ask too many questions and refuse to settle for stories and systems that are inherently unhealthy. It's a network of *healing justice* for survivors of misdiagnosis and overmedication, survivors of trauma, survivors of injustice. The Icarus Project advocates for an understanding of emotional struggle that acknowledges the impact of oppressive social forces. Inspired by the story of Icarus- the boy who flew too close to the sun with his wax wings- the original organizers envisioned a world where those who hear voices, see visions, and experience extreme sensitivities would be valued and understood as having "dangerous gifts," not mental diseases. The Icarus Project was foundational to my own healing process and helped me to widen my understanding of what holistic mental health looks like. Largely because of their influence, I was able to shift my own narrative from self-deprecation to self-empowerment, and embrace my sensitivities with curiosity. I led the Gainesville chapter for the Icarus Project for several years.

Also shortly after moving to Gainesville, I found myself sitting in a circle of LGBTQ students at a liberal Presbyterian bible study. The pastor, Reverend David Dean, read the story of Sodom and Gomorrah to us. This is the infamous text of the bible that is quoted by anti-gay fundamentalists who claim that God destroyed the two cities because of the supposed rampant homosexuality taking place there. Yet after Reverend Dean finished reading the story, he looked up and gently asked, "Does anyone hear anything about homosexuality in this story?" We didn't, because there is nothing about homosexuality in the story. In that moment, we all realized that the bible passage that for years has been used against the LGBTQ community is actually devoid of any anti-gay rhetoric. This realization shook our worlds. That was the whole bible study. For the remainder of the time, several of us just sat there and cried.

Ironically, the wealthy American evangelists that love to preach against "Sodomy" also love to ignore this verse of the bible: "Now this was the sin of your sister Sodom: She and her daughters were arrogant, overfed, and unconcerned; they did not help the poor and needy" (Ezekiel 16:49). The Presbyterian Student Center at the University of Florida became for me, and for many others, a place to heal from fundamentalism and to unlearn the harmful stories that we had been taught to believe. Through the influence of the Icarus Project, and the gentle guidance of Reverend David Dean, I was able to further deconstruct my reality and concretely shift my worldview.

Yet even after I let go of these constricting narratives, their influence still lived in my body, and still does in subtle ways. As one of my favorite authors, Raoul Vaneigem, said so strikingly about post-Christian Europe, "God has been abolished but the pillars which supported him still rise to an empty sky" (1983, p. 143). In order to truly embody a new story, we have to rid not only our minds but also our bodies of the old story, and intentionally practice a new way of being.

Practicing a New Reality

"The way you do anything is the way you do everything."

-Zen koan from Japan

It's been a stressful week and I haven't been sleeping well. As I have risen each morning, so have my eyebrows, wrinkling my forehead and widening my eyes. I've also been clenching my jaw and shortening my breath. Luckily I've noticed this pattern emerge and have made explicit efforts to reverse it. Doing so has shifted my mood and lowered my level of stress. When I feel crunched for time, as I have this week for various reasons, I crunch my shoulders, chest, and jaw. I tend to extend myself into the world quickly and rashly. It becomes difficult to take in or process what's happening around me because *there is no time!* My body tenses to block stimuli or new information. I exist in a kind of tunnel vision.

I have been proposing throughout this book that our bodies somatically organize in response to our environments. Our bodies take the shape of what we repeatedly do, and we are always doing something. This week, I have been unconsciously taking on the shape of stress. My awareness of this bodily habit has allowed me to take action to change it. The simple act of consciously lowering my eyebrows has effectively lowered my stress levels and allowed me to maintain the capacity to be aware and relaxed, as opposed to overwhelmed and reactive.

After interviewing someone for an administrative position in the government, President Abraham Lincoln turned to his assistant and said, "He's not the one. I don't like his face." Confused and surprised, the assistant asked Lincoln how he could not like someone simply because of their face. "After 40, everyone is responsible for their face," Lincoln replied (Strozzi-Heckler, 2007, p. 92).

The point of this tale, whether it's historically true or not, is that we are always practicing something, and what we practice shapes who we are.

> Because these practices are normally
> under the level of our conscious
> awareness it's understandable that this
> may seem subtle, but have no doubt that
> the way we somatically organize
> ourselves, moment by moment, shapes
> our worldview, and conversely this
> shapes how the world looks at us. The
> way we comport ourselves is a direct
> reflection of what we've been practicing.
> (Strozzi-Heckler, 2014, p. 76)

In this final chapter, I will mostly be drawing from the work and methodology of Richard Strozzi-Heckler and the Strozzi Institute, the organization that has been most foundational to my understanding of somatic awareness and practice. In 2016 I began training with the Strozzi Institute, starting with their 4-day *Introduction to Somatic Transformation*. I tend to stray away from making exaggerated statements, but the four days with the Strozzi Institute that I spent moving, shaking, and feeling the sensations in my body changed my life, and my understanding of life, profoundly.

The Strozzi Institute introduced me to the idea of somatic practice. If the repetition of actions, behaviors, moods, and movements, over time, become embodied and embedded in our musculature, then intentionally shifting our habits can fundamentally shift who we are and how we show up in the world. I explained in the last chapter how movement and habits, through repetition, become involuntary and unconscious. These habits often go unnoticed because we have learned, as a culture, to ignore sensations, to simply push through or block difficult bodily feelings. It takes courage and a change in perspective, accompanied by lots of intentional practice, to shift one's orientation back toward the body.

In a 2008 article titled *The Transformative Power of Practice* published by the Strozzi Institute, Staci Haines and Ng'ethe Maina make the distinction between *default* practices and *intentional* practices. Default practices are those behaviors and reactions that we embody without thinking. "Each time we practice piano with a grumpy attitude, then we may get better at piano, but we will also certainly get better at being grumpy" (2008, para. 4).

Reactionary habits are engrained in the psychobiology of our muscular system. Habitually moving away from those we have learned to fear, repeatedly crunching the forehead with stress, or even (physically) avoiding confrontation are examples of engrained reactions. These reactions become habitual and embodied over time if they are frequently repeated. They become our default practices. We have to establish new intentional practices to counteract these engrained habits. Yet in order to do this, we have to first become aware, somatically, of the patterns that we have embodied.

We learn to embody certain reactions based on our life experiences, perspectives, fears, hopes, and how we are oriented to the world. These learned patterns are not always inherently good or bad. We may have learned to react in certain ways as a defense mechanism that served us at a particular time in our lives. I vividly remember being terrified of my 1st grade teacher, a Catholic nun who smoked like a chimney in-between classes. If anyone asked her a question at the wrong moment, we could all feel wrath rising from her like steam. Her eyes would shoot beams of reprimand as she demanded that we not interrupt her again. I quickly learned not to speak up when I needed something. This was a useful protective habit that served me in that setting, yet to this day it's difficult for me to interrupt teachers or other authority figures to ask for what I need. When this fear reaction rises in my body in the form of shutting down, holding back, or freezing, I have to intentionally confront it, challenge it, and overcome it. Over the years, through practice and repetition, this has become easier. I still often notice a slight hesitation rise inside of me in these situations, yet I have become better at asking for what I need. These life experiences, especially if they are repeated frequently, are remembered by our bodies and affect our impulses and actions.

"It's important to remember that these moments that begin to define us are not disembodied thoughts or memories, but experiences that find a home in our musculature, voice, posture, in our very way of being" (Strozzi-Heckler, 2014, p. 74).

Our behaviors and attitudes, our moods and movement patterns, the way we view ourselves and the way we interact with others, are all the result of how our bodies react to information that is being triggered inside of us. As Sara Ahmed points out, "all actions are reactions" (2004, p. 5). Learning to be somatically aware of what's happening internally allows us to notice and respond to the feelings that are rising instead of simply reacting to them automatically and unconsciously. Learning to feel and observe bodily sensations gives us information about our learned patterns and default practices. If I am aware, for example, that I always cringe when my boss walks into the room, then I can begin to explore this pattern. Does is serve me? Does it hinder me? Where might I have learned this? Am I willing and able to practice a different reality when my boss walks into the room such as holding my own and standing in my power?

Meditation teaches the practitioner to "clear the mind" by noticing thoughts and letting them float by without becoming attached to them. Similarly, somatics teaches us to notice our feelings, to observe what's happening internally so that we can choose how and if to respond, instead of simply reacting. If we can become aware of and acquainted with our reactive tendencies, then we can practice a different response. When we cultivate the capacity to feel, to sit with uncomfortable sensation, and to not be immediately reactive, we increase our choice. Somatics, to a large extent, is about learning to take power back in order to not be controlled by historical tendencies and learned reactions.

In contrast, blocking feeling causes the energy of our biological reaction to stay in our bodies, constricting and shaping our muscles into patterns that hold the energy in. Opening the body to feeling allows this built up energy to be released and makes space for new responses. I will write more specifically about what this *somatic opening* can look like later in this chapter.

Attuning the attention to the sensations of the body and confronting habitual reactions is not particularly easy, but it is certainly transformative.

Bodily sensations can come in many forms. Surges of heat, coldness, numbness, tensing, subtle shakings, quiet quivering, or a quickened pulse. Noticing these feelings allows us to fully live in our bodies and to be connected with the deep longings and impulses that drive us toward life.

Strozzi-Heckler describes this as being "absorbed in the current of life awakening to itself." He goes on to say, "when we understand somatically how we have learned something; we have also learned how to unlearn something. This remarkably broadens and increases choice, and with that, responsibility" (2014, p. 53).

I once heard someone define responsibility as *maintaining the ability to respond*. This, to me, is what somatics is all about. Attuning our attention to the body and noticing what is coming up allows us to truly be present to ourselves and to others. Instead of reacting to the confusing streams of energy racing through our bodies, somatic awareness and practice allows us to notice, pause, and respond to the feelings and situations that life throws our way. Somatic awareness allows us to become aware of how we may be blocking feeling, love, and connection out of our lives by contracting our muscles. There are certainly times when blocking feeling is useful, as a matter of safety and protection, yet being aware of these blocks offers us the choice of whether we want them to remain intact or whether we want to shift them.

In order to transform our patterns and shift our habits, we have to practice a different reality. It's not enough to simply believe in a new reality, or to want a new reality. In order to embody a new way of being and responding, we have to practice. According to the Strozzi Institute, it takes about 300 repetitions for a new habit to become muscle memory and 3000 for it to become fully embodied.

Strozzi-Heckler says it this way:
We're inclined to lean on hope and

idealism that we, others, and societies
will change simply because we've been
introduced to a new idea. The
consequences of relying on hope without
new practices lead to a downward spiral
of frustration, resignation, and
hopelessness... Somatic practices allow
insights to become muscular
commitments to action. (2014, p. 76)

Let me give an example of what this embodied change process might look like. For many people, including myself, it's difficult to say no to commitments, even when we know it's impossible to follow through with them. This could stem from various things such as a fear of confrontation, or not wanting to hurt someone's feelings. So we over-commit, or say yes when we really want to say no.

As for myself, when I am confronted with an offer that I know I can't fulfill, I tend to softly decline, spouting out a million excuses and reasons why I can't say yes as if a simple "no thanks" is grossly insufficient. Shifting this tendency begins with noticing the sensations that arise when I am asked to over-commit or to do something that I don't want to do. What's happening in my body? Am I shrinking? Is my mind racing in search of excuses? Am I leaning backwards in hiding? Is my voice constricted making it difficult to assert myself? Or conversely, maybe I am leaning forward, ready to leap into a commitment I can't fulfill.

The second step to transforming this reaction is to fully allow those feelings to surface, and to gather the information about myself that is offered. I may not have realized that I tend to sink inward. Maybe I notice that the stream of excuses is flowing from a nervous anxiety located in the pit of my stomach. Personally, I know that in these situations I tend to shift my weight to my back. I may notice that this holding back feels protective, even as it hinders my ability to fully and confidently assert myself.

If I then decide that this pattern does not work for me, I can take steps to shift it. When confronted with a request I can't fulfill, I can consciously choose to orient my body in such a way that I am not holding back, or sinking inward. I can choose to stand in my power and to not let the stream of anxiety flow out my mouth in the form of excuses. Somatic awareness allows there to be a pause in the crucial moment between sensation and reaction. This is a moment of choice: will I fall into my default practice or will I intentionally practice a different way of being.

> Practice changes our minds, bodies, and moods towards a new way of being, because we are in fact momentarily living a new narrative, a new emotional orientation, and a new physical shape. Each time we do the practice, we are

> spending that moment of time
> interrupting the old habits and living the
> new pattern that we seek to put into
> place. Literally, as we practice new
> movements, internal conversations, and
> new emotional states, we are creating
> new neural pathways in the brain and
> new muscle memory in the body.
> (Haines and Maina, 2008, para. 15)

It's true that we are always practicing something, moment by moment, yet we don't have to wait for a challenge to occur in order to practice a new habit. We can design intentional practices that help us build resilience and muscle memory toward a new reality. The Strozzi Institute has created a series of somatic practices that are specifically intended to help people notice default habits and embody new ones. Strozzi's somatic methodology is about cultivating a strong and centered presence in the face of conflict and confrontation, and becoming aware of the bodily patterns and sensations that hinder this possibility. One such practice that I learned while training with the Strozzi Institute was specifically designed to help people embody the practice of saying "no" with dignity and confidence.

We split up into pairs of two. Person one stood still as person two voiced a request and then pointed at and moved toward person one. At first, I was person one. As my partner moved toward me, I was instructed to decline *with my whole body* by meeting my partner as they approached, saying "no," then turning their body around and gently, with my hands and full body force, guiding them away from me. This full-body practice of "declining" allowed me to notice any feelings, hesitancies, resistances, or overexertion that might have been present in my body while declining a request. It was quite revealing. There was hesitancy in my step and I placed my weight toward the back of my body, softening my force. This revealed what I had suspected it would: my tendency to hold back, to be extra gentle and non-assertive. Others noticed a tendency in themselves to be overbearing or forceful.

This practice also allows the person being declined to notice what it feels like to be told "no." When it was my turn to be declined, one of the teachers pointed out that it seemed as though I accepted the decline too easily. Instead of matching my partner's force and declining with dignity, I instead would turn around and walk away on my own, seemingly defeated. This was useful information about my default pattern.

This is just one example of the many intentional practices that the Strozzi Institute has created. Though the social setting of group practice is quite useful, somatic practice can also be done alone. Mindfulness and movement techniques such as meditation, yoga, Qi-Gong, and various forms of martial arts also have wonderful somatic benefits. Practicing stillness and slow, intentional movements, can reveal tendencies in the body that may be indicative of behavioral patterns. When practicing yoga for example, I may notice that I'm rushing the movements or holding my breath. This allows me to notice these tendencies, which may likely be present in other aspects of my life, and gives me a platform to practice transforming them.

Shifting Shape, Shifting Culture

In 1964, Brazil underwent the first in a series of tragic and deadly military coups. Augusto Boal, the director of the Arena Theatre in Sao Paulo at the time, began to envision a way that theatre could be used to empower the masses toward political rebellion. He created a revolutionary form of participatory community theatre that would eventually become known as Theatre of the Oppressed. Similar to Martin-Baro, Boal took a great degree of inspiration from Paulo Freire's concept of "awakening the critical consciousness" articulated in the now famous 1970 book, *Pedagogy of the Oppressed*.

Forum Theatre, the first major development of Boal's work, is a participatory method of theatre that erases the distinction between actors and audience. Through an initial conversation, the audience decides on a specific scene to act out that is relevant to a current or ongoing political struggle. The "actors" then play out this scene. If the portrayal of the events is unsatisfactory to anyone in the audience, they can yell "stop!" and replace any actor on stage, reworking the scene to their liking.

The idea behind this method is to provide a social forum for re-imagining responses to oppression by giving the community the opportunity to literally act out and embody various possibilities of liberation. This give the audience a chance to collectively work out solutions to a community problem, and empowers them to move from passive bystander to active participant in their own struggle. Theatre is somatically-oriented in that it requires a full-body form of participation. It is action-based, emphasizing the motions, expressions, and sensations of the stories being portrayed. Theatre creates the space to feel, embody, and practice solutions instead of simply brainstorming them. Boal states this connection clearly: "Theater is therapy into which one enters body and soul, soma and psyche" (Boal, 1995).

Shifting the body into a position of empowerment, even momentarily, has profound effects on the psyche. In her 2012 TED Talk that went viral, social psychologist Amy Cuddy explained an experiment she did in which she asked participants to pose for two minutes in various body stances. Hypothesizing that this brief period would bring about chemical changes in the brain, she tested the participant's testosterone and cortisol levels before and after the pose. Cuddy calls testosterone the "dominance chemical" and cortisol the "anxiety chemical." When participants were asked to stand in large, open, expressive postures, their testosterone levels increased and cortisol levels decreased. The exact opposite happened when participants were asked to stand or sit in contracted, closed off, or coiled up postures (Cuddy, 2012).

Theatre of the Oppressed is an inspiring example of how somatically-oriented techniques can be used for both individual and social transformation, empowering communities to embody a different story. Augusto Boal described this powerful work as one way "to free the body from the social distortion placed on it by the oppressor's ideological discourses" (Boal, 1974).

Generative Somatics, the non-profit partner of the Strozzi Institute, also uses somatic practices to empower political movements. They define somatics as a "practice-able theory of change that can move us toward individual, community, and collective liberation" (2016, para. 1).

I want to give voice to the inspiring and powerful work that Generative Somatics is doing by quoting them directly and at length:

> Somatics understands both the
> individual and collective as a
> combination of biological, evolutionary,
> emotional and psychological aspects,
> shaped by social and historical norms
> and adaptive to a wide array of both
> resilient and oppressive forces... A
> politicized somatic theory understands
> the need for deep personal
> transformation, aligned with liberatory
> community/collective practices,
> connected to transformative systemic
> change. One is inseparable from the next,
> and each should serve the other... a
> somatics without a political analysis of
> social institutions, unequal distribution
> of power and use of violence and force,
> leaves out some of the largest forces that
> shape us... A politicized somatics can act
> as a fundamental collective practice of
> building power, deepening presence and
> capacity, and developing the embodied
> skills we need to generate large-scale
> change. (2016, para. 6)

Generative Somatics brings embodied training practices into communities and organizations that are directly involved in, or impacted by, political struggle. These practices are designed to empower individuals and groups to become aware of the sensations, tendencies, and historically embodied habits that hinder growth and transformation, and to move past them by building resilience. This transformative somatic work begins deep inside the organs, tissues, and fascia of the individual and expands outward into the social body.

Often the first step to embodying change is to heal the deep wounds of individual and collective trauma. Generative Somatics puts a great emphasis on this particular piece of transformative work. The oppressive forces of society shape our bodies, and so often this leaves scars. Accessing deep emotions and memories can be terrifying and triggering, especially for historically marginalized groups.

Moving Beyond Triggers

Staci Haines, co-director of the Strozzi Institute and founder of Generative Somatics believes that the effects of trauma can be healed, and that the painful memories that rise in our bodies can be helpful guides to this healing process. In other words, she believes that gently, slowly, yet fully feeling into uncomfortable sensations and triggers can create an opening that leads the way towards resilience and healing.

A negative view of triggers sees them as inevitable, as a sort of inherited flaw in our psyche that limits our ability to move through the world, making us victims to the past. A somatics view of triggers sees them as insights into pieces of ourselves that are in need of attention. This is not meant to downplay the pain; it's meant to redirect it so it can be healed.

When witnessing or experiencing traumatic events, the body shifts into a hyper-arousal state. We use all of our energy to pump blood into the larger action muscles, which speeds the heart rate, raises blood pressure, and either accelerates breathing or tightens the lungs. Non-survival functions such as hunger, sleep, and digestion are shut down to preserve energy for fight or flight. When the body, in its instinctual wisdom, perceives that neither fighting nor fleeing is possible, it freezes and dissociates, releasing painkilling endorphins and opioids, and shutting down muscle function until the threat is over.

When the threat passes, the body then knows how to return to balance. There is often an immediate impulse to cry, scream, jump, shake, tremble, or sweat. This is the body's way of releasing the excess stress chemicals and shifting out of hyper-arousal mode.

Yet if these chemicals are not released and the body does not shift back to a state of regulation, the experience does not leave the body. It stays. In the interest of "never feeling that way again" we learn to contract our muscles in ways that block the release every time it comes up, every time we are triggered.

> Triggers are history seeping out through
> the present, pieces of memory emerging
> from the past. While the pain, anger, or
> confusion can seem to be a response to
> something that is happening today, it is
> really a fragment of visual, emotional, or
> body memory making its way to the
> surface. Triggers act like cracks in
> present day reality that open to
> unresolved trauma from the past.
> (Haines, 2007, p. 83)

Somatically speaking, triggers are bodily signs of unresolved trauma, of unreleased traumatic energy that needs to come out. Through somatic practices, "we access the traumatic contractions, help them to soften, and support the psychobiological release. This in turn changes one's sense of self, who one is in relationship, and opens choices and new actions" (Haines, 2007, p. xix).

A former teacher of mine at the Florida School of Massage, Michael Broas, once told a story that illustrates this idea. When he was a solider in Vietnam, there were several life threatening situations from which he wanted to run away. Yet in almost all of those situations, because of the terrain and spaciousness of the land, there was literally nowhere to run. Michael instead froze, fearing for his life. Decades later, while attending a workshop on PTSD, Michael's legs began shaking as he was recalling memories of war. The workshop facilitator encouraged him to let it

117

happen, so he did, and his legs shook erratically for a full 90 minutes. Michael explained that because he was unable to run in Vietnam, the mobilizing energy was never fully released from the body. This traumatic energy was buried deep inside Michael's legs, rising to the surface decades later once it was finally allowed to.

In regards to sexual abuse, Staci Haines makes an extraordinary claim that displays the changing paradigm of trauma studies: "Once you have released the trauma from the area of your body where the trigger is stored and have processed the experience emotionally, the trigger will fade" (1999, p. 151).

> She goes on to say explain: Avoiding triggers leaves all of the landmines of sexual abuse in place, so the terrain of your life continues to feel dangerous and untrustworthy. When triggers are taken on, felt, and processed, they shrink or transform altogether. What was once a trigger becomes a completed part of your history. You may notice it periodically, but it no longer runs you. (1999, p. 156)

This can of course be an extremely scary confrontation and often requires a safe space and trained facilitator. Yet it is also true that this energy can sometime release spontaneously. Whenever or wherever this release happens, it's useful to have a framework for what is going on. Psychotherapist and trauma expert Pat Ogden refers to these biological releases as "Sensorimotor Sequencing."

> This is how she explains it: Sensorimotor Sequencing is a trauma processing technique that allows the patient to re-activate a 'sliver' of traumatic memory in a mindful dual awareness and then facilitate the completion of the movements and sensations and responses that arise… allowing them to unfold moment by moment until they spontaneously complete or transform. (Ogden, 2001)

Somatics is about resilience. As I've been suggesting, contrary to popular rhetoric, feeling your emotions actually gives you power and choice. Ignoring feelings limits your capacity to thoughtfully respond to life's challenges. Opening the body to feeling is the first step to healing, transformation, and cultivating the emotional capacity to move through difficult moments with resilience and power. The practice of remaining centered and open allows new trauma, pain, and oppressive forces to move through the body, completing the full biological cycle of activation and release, instead of getting stuck and buried within. This opens the pathway to resilience, to truly embodying a position of empowerment. If we are closed off, we either block feeling completely or we chronically hold feeling inside. If we are open somatically, we are able to let feelings pass through, take from them what we want, and respond thoughtfully instead of reactively.

> Trauma researcher and founder of the *Somatic Experiencing* technique, Peter Levine, offers this encouragement: the same immense energies that create the symptoms of trauma, when properly engaged and mobilized, can transform the trauma and propel us into new heights of healing, mastery, and even wisdom. Trauma resolved is a great gift, returning us to the natural world of ebb and flow, harmony, love, and compassion. We humans have the innate capacity to heal not only ourselves, but our world, from the debilitating effects of trauma. (Levine, 1997)

Opening My Heart

The foundational practice that the Strozzi Institute teaches is called *Centering*. The Strozzi method of centering focuses on bodily dimensions of height, width, and depth. The idea is to learn to fully open the body, to expand in a way that promotes the free flow of feeling. In order to avoid feeling we often tend to contract inward, very subtly. Over time, the body learns this shape and organizes the muscular system and fascia to hold that insular position, blocking impulse and emotion, or holding it all in. It takes practice to train the body to stay open, to feel, to have a "sense" of one's internal and external world.

I was taught this practice of centering during the first training that I attended with the Strozzi Institute and have been utilizing it in my daily life ever since. They encouraged us to practice centering at least five times a day. The basics of the practice are as follows:

a. Stand with your feet shoulder width apart, eyes open, body fully relaxed.

b. Shift your attention from "the thinking self to the feeling self," noticing pressure, temperature, internal movement, etc.

c. Stand in your length, or "dignity": feel grounded and rooted through your feet while fully lengthening your spine upward toward the sky.

d. Expand in your full width, into the "relational space": You can either stretch your arms out from your sides or imagine your shoulders beaming outward to fully unfurl from life's constant pressure to shrink up. Expand into the world and the community around you.

    e. Settle into your depth, or "deep internal landscape": Notice if you are leaning forward or backwards and instead try to center your weight between the front and back of your feet. Connect to your past history by feeling into your back muscles. Next, feel into your capacity to lovingly expand into the future by bringing your attention to the sensations of your chest and front side.

Before I learned the Strozzi Institute method of centering I had been utilizing a different method that I learned from a Qi-Gong teacher. I was first introduced to this practice nearly a decade ago. I remember it vividly because my initial experience of practicing it was quite profound. We were instructed to close our eyes and scan our bodies, from head to toe, one section at a time. As I moved my attention between the regions of my body, each subsequent section began to relax. I had been holding extreme amounts of tension, yet I hadn't ever realized this partly because I hadn't ever taken the time to notice. At that point in my life, I had been struggling with prostate problems and often carried a lot of pain in my sacral region. Once my attention arrived at this area, I felt a release so loud that I heard a crack and I nearly fell over. I had been holding unthinkable amounts of tension, yet had been totally unaware. Literally, all I had to do was notice it, and it dissolved. A combination of this body-scanning practice and Strozzi's method of centering has become my foundational daily practice.

My first experience of utilizing the Strozzi Institute's centering practice during their 4-day training was also profound. I realized that I don't typically embody my full length, from top to bottom. I tend to shorten my spine by tilting my head slightly back, which pulls my shoulders forward and closes my ribcage. When I lengthened my spine and "stood in my height" it opened my chest, and I experienced a stream of energy moving through my body so strongly that it nearly caused me to panic. I had apparently been blocking this energetic flow unknowingly.

After we were taught to center we were told to pair up. I was instructed to stand still, fully centered, and to think about something that I care deeply about. My partner was then instructed to slowly place his hand on my chest, contacting my heart, and to apply a slowly increasing pressure. As he did this, my heart began to race and I completely dissociated. I couldn't think or move. I froze, completely checking out of reality.

On that third day of the training, as I was processing this with one of the teachers, he told me that I likely hold a lot of tension in my chest area, my heart center. I told him about the community mental health work I am involved with, how I support others by listening to their stories of pain and trauma. He asked me if I tend to "take on" other people's pain. Before my brain could answer the question, my body spoke with a resounding yes, and the tears began to stream out. We hugged and I went into the restroom to "let it all out." I trembled. I convulsed. I cried and I cried. And then I felt noticeably different. I felt alive.

During the training I had made space in my body for deeply suppressed emotions to surface. Once I began to notice these sensations and allowed myself to feel them, I experienced what the Strozzi Institute calls a *somatic opening*. I felt an immediate sense of relief and weightlessness. When I spoke up in the group my heart was no longer racing. I could assert my voice into the ether with confidence and power. The contraction in my chest had been released, and I have since been practicing a different shape, one that allows this emotional energy to flow and be felt, instead of stagnate and get stuck.

This experience was transformative, but it wasn't the end of this pattern. I still tend to hold energy in my chest. I still have a tendency to close my heart, to block feelings of connection, to hide inward in learned patterns of shame, insecurity, and fear. Yet now that I am aware of this pattern, I have the power to change it. Transformation is an ongoing practice.

Moving Forward

As I mentioned in chapter one, my early days as a body-worker set the stage for my ongoing curiosity of this complex, dynamic, ever-shifting organism we call body. It became glaringly clear to me that emotional content lives within the tissues of muscles, and that this content, often buried and forgotten, likely has something to say.

Just as Ignacio Martin-Baro became an outspoken critic of the individualistic-orientation of Western psychology, I quickly became frustrated with the individualistic-orientation of massage therapy. Week after week, clients would come to me with stress-related ailments from work, relationships, trauma, etc., and I would help their body's reset temporarily so they could return to their problematic situations, and then return to me the next week. It was too far out of my scope of practice for me to address the underlying issues that were screaming so loudly through their muscles and trigger points. I had no idea how to address them anyway.

I longed for a deeper and lasting transformation that would reach beyond the individual body and touch into the social situations that shape bodies. One day in massage school, a teacher mentioned somatics and suggested that this type of transformative work is indeed possible. I distinctly remember the very feeling that flooded by body and filled my senses with wonder. I ran up to the teacher after class, begging to know more. He suggested a few authors: Wilhelm Reich, Alexander Lowen, and Ron Kurtz. Within two weeks I had read every book by these authors I could get my hands on. I have been following this same impulse for years now with undying curiosity.

The years that I have since spent researching, writing, moving, training, thinking, and dreaming, have allowed me to turn this curious inquiry into a practice-able knowledge of the somatic process. I have been able to access the stories that live inside my own musculature and work towards shifting my personal reality. And I have begun to discover how body-work, somatic practices, movement, theatre, and other such modalities can be used to help others access these stories as well. I am learning that somatics has a unique and profound ability to transform lives, communities, and worlds. As my exploration of the social body continues to grow and develop, I will be focusing much of my attention on how individual and collective somatic practices can be used to facilitate broad and lasting social transformation.

Bodies organize in response to our environments. Stories, beliefs, and experiences shape our bodies in the form of movement patterns, habits, impulses, and feeling reactions. Our personal stories can either be a source of empowerment or a source of limitation. An embodied critical examination of these narratives, forces, and feelings opens the possibility of transformation on both a micro and macro level. Somatic work is not simply about opening the body to feeling; it's about creating the resources that we need in order to navigate life from a place of responsiveness and integrity. Learning to feel what's happening in the body allows us the opportunity to practice new patterns of being that support growth, centeredness, and transformation. As we transform ourselves, we strengthen our capacity to effectively take action toward the creation of what Ignacio Martin-Baro envisioned: 'healthy, free, and creative minds' in a 'free, dynamic, and just social body'" (2008, p. 25).

Bibliography

Ahmed, S. (2015). *The cultural politics of emotion* (Second edition). New York: Routledge.

Ahmed, S. (2008). *Queer phenomenology: orientations, objects, others*. Durham: Duke University Press.

Boal, A. (1985). *Theatre of the oppressed*.

Boal, A. (1995). *The rainbow of desire: the boal method of theatre and therapy*. London ; New York: Routledge.

Butler, J. (1993). *Bodies that matter: on the discursive limits of "sex."* New York: Routledge.

Cuddy, A. (2012, June). Amy Cuddy: *Your Body Language Shapes Who You Are* [Video file]. Retrieved from http://www.ted.com/talks/amy_cuddy_your_body_langua ge_shapes_who_you_are#t-738545

Damasio, A. R. (1994). *Descartes' error: emotion, reason, and the human brain*. New York: Putnam.

Elkind, D., (1971). *Wilhelm reich: the psychoanalyst as revolutionary*. New York Times.

Frye, M. (1983). *The politics of reality: essays in feminist theory*. Trumansburg, N.Y: Crossing Press.

Generative Somatics (2016). *What is a politicized somatics?* Retrieved from http://www.generativesomatics.org/content/theory-what-politicized-somatics

Haines, S., Newman, F., & Haines, S. (2007). *Healing sex: a mind-body approach to healing sexual trauma* (Updated 2nd ed). San Francisco: Cleis Press.

Haines, S., Maina, N. (2008). *The transformative power of practice*. Retrieved from http://strozziinstitute.com/articles/the-transformative-power-of-practice/

Hanna, T. (1970). *Bodies in revolt; a primer in somatic thinking* (1st ed.). New York: Holt, Rinehart and Winston.

Hanna, T. (1988*). Somatics: reawakening the mind's control of movement, flexibility, and health.* Reading, Mass: Addison-Wesley.

Hanna, T., (1986, April 9). *What is somatics*. SOMATICS: Magazine-Journal of the Bodily Arts and Sciences, V, 4, Spring/Summer.

Harper, D. (n.d.). Online Etymology Dictionary. Retrieved June 21, 2016, from http://etymonline.com/index.php?allowed_in_frame=0 In American Heritage Dictionary online. Retrieved from https://ahdictionary.com/word/search.html?q=impulse

Impulse. (n.d.). In Merriam-Webster Dictionary online. Retrieved from http://www.merriam-webster.com/dictionary/impulse

James, W. (1995a). *The principles of psychology: in two volumes. Vol. 2: [...]*. New York: Dover.
Johnson, D. (1983). *Body*. Boston: Beacon Press.

Keleman, S. (1985). *Emotional anatomy: the structure of experience.* Berkeley, Calif.: Center Press.

Kierkegaard, S., (2002). *The Crowd is Untruth. In On the Dedication to "That Single Individual".* Retrieved from http://oregonstate.edu/instruct/phl201/modules/Philosoph ers/Kierkegaard/kierkegaard_the_crowd_is_untruth.html

Kurtz, R., & Prestera, H. (1976). *The body reveals: an illustrated guide to the psychology of the body* (1st ed). New York: Harper & Row/Quicksilver Books.

Levine, B. E. (2014, November). Why an assassinated psychologist - ignored by US psychologists - is being honored. *Truthout.* Retrieved from http://www.truth- out.org/opinion/item/27244-why-an-assassinated- psychologist-ignored-by-us-psychologists-is-being- honored

Levine, P. A. (1997). *Waking the tiger: healing trauma: the innate capacity to transform overwhelming experiences.* Berkeley, Calif: North Atlantic Books.
Lowen, A. (1973). *Depression and the body: the biological basis of faith and reality.* Baltimore: Penguin.

Macnaughton, I. (Ed.). (2004). *Body, breath & consciousness: a somatics anthology: a collection of articles on family systems, self-psychology, the bodynamics model of somatic developmental psychology, shock trauma, and breathwork.* Berkeley, Calif: North Atlantic Books.

Marcher, L., & Fich, S. (2010). *Body encyclopedia: a guide to the psychological functions of the muscular system*. Berkeley, Calif: North Atlantic Books.

Marlock, G., Weiss, H., Young, C., Soth, M., & Society for the Study of Native Arts and Sciences (Eds.). (2015). *The handbook of body psychotherapy and somatic psychology*. Berkeley, California: North Atlantic Books.

Martín-Baró, I., Aron, A., & Corne, S. (1994). *Writings for a liberation psychology*. Cambridge, Mass: Harvard University Press.

Mehl-Madrona, L. (2007). *Narrative medicine: the use of history and story in the healing process*. Rochester, Vt: Bear & Co.

Merleau-Ponty, M., & Lefort, C. (1968). *The visible and the invisible: followed by working notes*. Evanston: Northwestern University Press.

Osborne, R., & Edney, R. (2007). *Philosophy for beginners* (Reprint ed). Danbury, CT: For Beginners LLC.

Poulette, R. (2012, Winter). *Bend the rules*. Geez Magazine, 33.

Rapoport, J. L. (1991). *The boy who couldn't stop washing: the experience and treatment of obsessive compulsive disorder* (1. Signet print). New York: Signet Books.

Reich, W. (1990). *Character analysis*. New York: Noonday Press.

Reich, W., Higgins, M., & Raphael, C. M. (1993). *The mass psychology of fascism*. New York: Noonday Press.

Rothschild, B. (2000). *The body remembers: the psychophysiology of trauma and trauma treatment*. New York: Norton

Strozzi-Heckler, R. (2007). *The leadership dojo: build your foundation as an exemplary leader*. Berkeley, Calif: Frog, Ltd. ; Distributed by North Atlantic books.

Strozzi-Heckler, R. (2014). *The art of somatic coaching: embodying skillful action, wisdom, and compassion*. Berkeley, California: North Atlantic Books.

Watkins, M., & Shulman, H. (2010*). Toward psychologies of liberation*. Basingstoke: Palgrave Macmillan.

Vaneigem, R., & Nicholson-Smith, D. (1983). *The revolution of everyday life*. Seattle; Welcombe, England: Left Bank Books ; Rebel Press.

Vygotskij, L. S., & Cole, M. (1981). *Mind in society: the development of higher psychological processes* (Nachdr.). Cambridge, Mass.: Harvard Univ. Press.

About the Author

Rusti Poulette is a licensed massage therapist and a practitioner of somatics living in Gainesville, Florida. Rusti has a B.A. in Health Arts and Sciences (somatics concentration) through Goddard College and will soon be pursuing a Master's Degree in Embodiment Studies.

Rusti is also a Theatre of the Oppressed facilitator and is currently training with the Strozzi Institute and Generative Somatics. The world is Rusti's preferred classroom: the open road, the energy of cities, the freedom of pine forests, salt-water baptisms, poetry scribbled into wrinkled journals, DIY music, improvised noise, and the constant lessons learned through conversations and connections with friends near and far.

Rusti is available to facilitate transformational workshops for activist collectives and other groups. These movement-based, interactive workshops are designed to strengthen affinity among participants and promoting somatic awareness.

More information and more of Rusti's writing can be found at
RustiPoulette.com

www.ingramcontent.com/pod-product-compliance
Lightning Source LLC
Chambersburg PA
CBHW072053280526
45788CB00006B/2275